VOICE IN THE AMERICAN WEST

Andy Wilkinson
Series Editor

LIGHT
IN THE TREES

For Annette,
& your own High Valley
memories, & in appreciation
for your Support —
Gail Folkins

Light in the Trees

Gail Folkins

Foreword by Andy Wilkinson

Texas Tech University Press

This book is typeset in Perrywood MT. The paper used in this book meets the minimum requirements of ANSI/NISO Z39.48-1992 (R1997). ∞

Designed by Ashley Beck
Cover designed by Kasey McBeath

Library of Congress Cataloging-in-Publication Data
Names: Folkins, Gail Louise, 1963– | Wilkinson, Andy, writer of foreword.
Title: Light in the trees / Gail Folkins ; foreword by Andy Wilkinson.
Description: Lubbock, Texas : Texas Tech University Press, 2016. | Series: Voice in the American West | Includes bibliographical references.
Identifiers: LCCN 2015028621| ISBN 9780896729513 (hardback) | ISBN 9780896729520 (paperback) | ISBN 9780896729537 (e-book)
Subjects: LCSH: Folkins, Gail Louise, 1963—Family. | Folkins, Gail Louise, 1963—Homes and haunts. | Washington (State)—Description and travel. |Northwest, Pacific—Description and travel. | Natural history—Northwest, Pacific. | City and town life—Northwest, Pacific. | Lifestyles—Northwest, Pacific. | BISAC: BIOGRAPHY & AUTOBIOGRAPHY /Personal Memoirs. | NATURE / Essays.
Classification: LCC PS3606.O455 Z46 2016 | DDC 814/.6—dc23
LC record available at http://lccn.loc.gov/2015028621

16 17 18 19 20 21 22 23 24 / 9 8 7 6 5 4 3 2 1

Texas Tech University Press
Box 41037 | Lubbock, Texas 79409-1037 USA
800.832.4042 | ttup@ttu.edu
www.ttupress.org

For my family

The wonder is that we can see these trees and not wonder more.
Ralph Waldo Emerson

Contents

Contents

FOREWORD

The editor's job is the same as the writer's job. Each must be master of the whole glass of water, first and foremost to extoll the fullness of the glass, and only afterwards to address the remaining emptiness. The difference betwixt the two is that the writer's audience is the reader while the editor's audience is the writer. This is not to say that the work of either writer or editor is to provide a full glass—were that even possible—for the joy of writing and the joy of reading is the same: the personal exploration of the surrounding world. In this sense, it is well to think of both writer and editor as mentors in the way described by novelist Max Evans, who holds that mentors are not simply teachers but guides who show their proteges the world into which they are entering. Once inside, the work is all up to the protege, whether reader or writer.

The job undertaken by the writer of a foreword, or an introduction or a preface, is the exception that tests the rule of such sweeping generalizations as these. It is a job that is neither the editor's nor the writer's. By now it is too late to influence the writer in their work, and the readers who are to come, quite rightly, belong to the writer. Yet the rule stands, for this is also a job of mentoring, providing the reader with a look into the world of the book into which they are about to enter.

Gail Folkins is an essayist, which is a way of saying that she has a poet's heart and a journalist's mind. And as with others of her kind, the two are in constant competition for control of her voice. In her first book—*Texas Dance Halls: A Two-Step Circuit*—it was her journalistic voice that triumphed as she followed her bass-playing husband and his band across the state's Hill Country, accompanied by photographer J. Marcus Weekley. The combination of the two sets of eyes—that of a visual artist along with a journalist—resulted in a photo-essay that documented the intertwined lives of the musicians and the dancers and the halls themselves. Speaking through the journalist's voice, Gail was neither participant nor historian, but rather the outsider looking in, all the while bringing the reader along with her in the exploration of a culture and its long story without pro-scribing it or defining it.

In this, her second book—written in a similar manner though tackling a broader, less defined subject—Gail is no longer the outsider, but rather the insider looking out, inviting the reader into the journey that she makes from the place of her forming to the places of her re-forming. Described as "a memoir of home, nature, and change in the American West," *Light in the Trees* is plainly intended to be personal history, but it reads equally as a series of closely-related essays, the whole seasoned with facts drawn from the larger history of the America that lies between Texas and the Pacific Northwest. Unlike her first work, *Light in the Trees* deals with a more complex subject matter, one without a simple, unified story, and one without the photographs that served as visual commentary in the earlier book. The difference makes a stronger and more adventurous work, the kind of work that requires the poet's voice.

That is the fullness of the glass. What about the emptiness? It is this: neither the poet's heart nor the journalist's mind can do the reader's job. A true mentor, the essayist merely shows the reader the glass. It remains for the reader to fill it, which is a good job to have.

Andy Wilkinson
Lubbock, Texas
2015

LIGHT IN THE TREES

Prologue

I floated from a rope swing above a mountain-cold creek and a ravine covered in ferns. The swing, fixed high and strong by my dad to a gray-spotted alder, offered a gentle bounce but nothing more on its back and forth glide, slow and measured as summer. Grade-school age and seated on a round, plywood disc, I swung my feet on what felt like a long-distance journey over the creek, the footbridge, and a trail on the other side of the creek wandering through cedar, hemlock, and Douglas fir. The twenty-five-foot rope length gave the swing a slow-as-molasses drift between the steadfastness of the bridge and clouds backlit by the sun, between the solidity of the moment and what came next. It was the same filtered light I'd follow on hikes up the mountain and, eventually, beyond it.

In my mid-twenties, I moved to Central Texas, its green hills and velvet wind giving me not only a new landscape to learn but also a sharper sense of where I'd grown up. From a backyard in Austin under a decades-old pecan tree, I wrote my way back to the creek's chattering cold and the warm breath of the horses I rode on neighboring Cougar Mountain. Several years later, a chance to attend graduate school in West Texas helped refine my writing. Shaded by a sycamore tree and a wider sky than I'd ever known, I filled the ample space with essays about a newspaper job, Squak Mountain, and a volcano. The only sound on those long afternoons, other than the wind, was the sycamore tree bouncing seed pods onto the roof of the yellow house we lived in, each thump random and surprising as memory.

After finishing school and returning to Austin, I started writing about more recent travels to the Northwest. With the distance of both geography and time, each summer and winter stay in the region revealed something new about this familiar terrain, whether changeable weather, uneasy geography, or new migration patterns for area wildlife. Many of these shifts mirrored the human impact on the natural world in other parts of the West, a landscape tangled in growth, change, and preservation efforts. In addition to highlighting place, each trip back also revealed the landscape of family and its steady, but sometimes sudden, changes over time.

When I finished drifting over the trees, I waited for the swing to shorten its unhurried motion just enough to hop onto the bridge. I was careful to prop the swing's wooden seat just beneath the bridge railing so it'd be ready for the next traveler, whether me, my brother Ken, or one of our friends. I stepped off the bridge and onto the worn, uphill trail toward the house, stopping at a huckleberry bush partway up. Growing from a moss-stained stump, the huckleberry's oval leaves formed a bonsai-perfect shape sprinkled with salmon-pink berries ready to sample. I tasted one of the tart, rounded berries and clasped a few more, sharp keepsakes for the rest of the way.

1

BLACKBERRY SUMMERS

In a clearing fierce with stickers, we hunted for berries, nevermind the vines scratching our wrists or seed balls stuck to our ankles. The blackberries my older brother Ken and I picked grew wild in unexpected places. Tangled in canopies reaching for the sun, the patches we scoured had taken over this area logged years before. Still, only a few berries lined the bottom of my colander. It shouldn't have taken much to fill such a small container, but there were leaves to get past, sharp berries to taste, the breeze to feel. At seven years old, I stood under the tall brambles, tasted another defiant berry, and tried to keep up with Ken.

Both of us were freckled and skinny, but from there all similarities ended—we were five years and a foot apart. Ken had wavy, brown hair, while mine was thin, light, and straight. Unlike my colander, his was half full, enough to not hear berries plunking against the metal bottom. He slipped between the vines, blending in with his green shirt and dark curls until I couldn't see him at all in this place locked in time.

Ken was the one who found berries in old clearings like this one near our grandma's house in rural western Washington, on patches of land thinned for roads and new construction. I imagined the trees coming back in years to come, although the berries, rather than promoting forest growth, sometimes prevented it. The smaller berries were native to the area; the thicker berry, the Himalayan, was probably introduced from Europe. Family on our Mom's side, three generations back, took root just as fast.

Born in Illinois, our maternal great-great-grandfather, James Knox Bailey, traveled in a great arc across the Midwest. His children, born in Illinois, Iowa, Missouri, Arkansas, Kansas, and Oklahoma, pinpoint his journey along the way. Family stories say he farmed and hunted in Kansas "until that state became settled too thick." He tried living in Texas, but disliking it, returned to Kansas. Torn between Indian Territory and the

Pacific Northwest, he chose Washington State, and in 1883 moved his family by train to San Francisco and by boat to a remote area of Pacific County he named Paradise Ranch.

Ten of James Bailey's children helped take care of the land and the log house with cedar siding. Sisters Mary and Olive hauled water from a stream and hiked two miles to get the mail from the nearest settlement. The children's role at the homestead grew when James Bailey's wife, Mary Ray, died four years later. The youngest daughter, Mary, described one summer where she had one dress and no shoes. A few of the family members traveled east of the Cascade Mountains to find work, most likely in the fruit orchards.

In the berry thicket, Mom's fingers moved through the vines with ease, her colander almost as full as Ken's. She and my brother picked alike through quick actions, sparse words, and few worries, at least none they voiced out loud. Mom's hair, the same color as mine but wavy rather than straight, stayed hidden in the berry patch until it was hard to tell where her hair started and the vines began. She stared at my stained hands. "You'd better save some for picking," she said, her words mild, no bite to them.

The sky was blue as a child's crayon. I parted the miniature leaves of another vine, green with red edges, and stuck my hands into the purple barbs. The vines twisted overhead and reached for our arms, which bore their random pink scratches. In this shadowy cluster, I couldn't blame the berries for wanting to stay, their tangled reach for secret clearings and rare sunshine.

Ken, his container now full, smirked at my near-empty colander and shook his head. He plucked each berry as if his fingers remembered something my meandering ones didn't.

At Grandma's house, Mom and Ken's containers brimmed to the top, while my berries sloped against the edges yet dipped in the center, a pretend fullness. Grandma, whose smaller bowl was also full, smiled without lingering on my half-empty colander. She was petite, like Mom, her fingers tough and small, her expression soft. Staying on the edge of the brambles, she'd still picked more berries than me, but was just as happy watching them ripen, content with the blackberries to stay whether they belonged here or not.

Mom piled the berries together until it didn't matter anymore. To celebrate our afternoon picking, she measured ingredients for blackberry pie, my favorite. After rolling the dough paper thin, she dusted it in flour, setting squares of butter in the middle. I didn't hear the rain start to fall, didn't see the sky darken. Purple juice oozing through the crust was more distracting, luring me from sibling rivalry to the sweeter home those berries made.

During summer storms, wind blustered across a plastic tarp on Grandma's front windows, making haunted-house sounds in the middle of the night. I buried my face in a blanket and tried to drown out these loud whispers, sure to be the distant sigh of those who lived here before: loggers, farmers, and miners. Charles Bailey, my great-grandfather, worked as a logger near the town of Elma. He was a bucker, someone who waited for a tree to fall with a ground-shaking *whump* and then sliced it into shorter logs to feed the waiting sawmills. It was dangerous work because of the unpredictable ways a tree might fall or roll. An oral account from his sister, Mary, tells how hard her big brother worked, how rarely the younger ones saw him, though he always had candy for them at Christmas. Mary remembers Charles marrying Anna Maas in 1894, when Mary was seven years old. Her father served as justice of the peace and played music after the ceremony, violin notes floating into the trees.

The floor creaked; from who or what, I wasn't sure. Grandma and Grandpa's room was only a few doorways from where I slept, but I was too embarrassed to wake them. Once I stood in their bedroom, past stories and immediate fears would fade in the reasoned light of their bedside lamp. Mom slept in a small bedroom off the kitchen, still warm from the potbellied stove in the corner. I used to share her double bed until she tired of my restless dreams and set me up on a comfortable mattress near the kitchen, a space that kept me in the middle of things. Ken, oblivious to quivering trees and rattling plastic, snored on the couch. He turned and didn't stir again. If I woke him now, a teasing was all I'd get.

Grandma's house turned friendly by morning, sunlight shining onto faded wallpaper and a gnome with red shoes and a green suit smiling wide-eyed and vacant from the flower bed outside. Grandpa Craig shuffled past my mattress on his way to the bathroom, and Grandma poked the kindling, small pieces of the forest crackling with cedar scent and sparking in the stove.

I threw on the yellow shirt and red pants Mom had sewn for me and stepped outside. Maybe we'd walk to the lake today and feed the ducks, the squawking birds circling us against a backdrop of reeds taller than I was. I'd toss bread toward each gaping beak, family members jostling for space.

Mary's account tells of her own sibling rivalry, how she and her sister Olive fought over a pan of water after a hot day helping their father burn brush. Olive reached the water first, banging her head on the way. Mary taunted her, saying, "Goody." That did it for Olive, who chased her younger sister and dumped the water, which both of them hauled every day, on top of Mary's head.

Something clanked in the detached garage, Ken wheeling Grandma's bicycle from the darkened shed onto the sidewalk. Chin thrust out in a challenge, he pointed the bike toward the gate. Even though the bike had three wheels and a large basket in the back of it, my brother handled it like a sports car.

Mom watched him from Grandma's backyard, her feet in the flowerbed and her gloved hands gliding through rosebushes instead of blackberries. "Is your sister going with you?" she asked. She probably thought having me along would make Ken go slower, although the opposite was true.

The screen door stuttered closed after Grandma, who'd traded her bathrobe for jeans and a short-sleeved shirt. She smiled at Ken and told him, "Have fun." She didn't seem to notice the competitive edge to our activities, or maybe she ignored it, just as she'd looked past the quiet disagreements of my mom and her younger sister, Delores. Without a word, Grandma joined Mom near the gnome, both of them coaxing pastel blooms from moist dirt.

Later in life, Charles Bailey became a gardener, replacing the trees he'd felled with flowers and shrubs. The years of the lone logger cutting solitary trees were waning, displaced by harvests fueled with mechanization, efficiency, and speed. During the last years of Charles's life, his wife committed him to a home after he started a fire, whether in the house or outside wasn't clear. Mom wondered if it was an accident, if her grandmother made up her mind too quickly.

"C'mon," Ken said. He walked the glistening bike through the gate and latched it behind us.

Saying no wasn't an option. I climbed into the basket and sat back-to-back with Ken, facing the road behind us. With fingers curled around the wire basket frame, I felt, rather than saw, my brother's legs pushing the bike past Grandma's picket fence and into the alley. Within view of the adults, our pace stayed slow. I waved at Grandma, Mom, and the gnome.

Ken rang the bike bell, its sound shrill like a warning. Past neighboring yards, he pedaled faster, blurring skinny pickets and sweeping by trim houses full of their own family stories. My brother's eyes narrowed against the wind. "Hang on," he growled.

Bike tires skidded, dipping into a ditch before coming back up. The sun poked thin streaks between the clouds, a chilly day by most standards but sunny for us. We scooted up and down more ditches; my teeth clenched when the basket screeched and bounced. Trees blurred; the small houses multiplied. I wouldn't let my nerves get the best of me, any more than Mary did on her trips to get the mail two miles through the woods on a narrow trail punctuated with a human skull someone set on a log.

"Hang on, weakling!" Ken hollered. While my hair stood out like scattered straw, his blew in waves lapping the air behind him. We zoomed under rows of telephone poles that had once been trees, wires from their branchless trunks sagging and tangled as blackberry vines, unruly as our hair.

After dinner, the television snapped to life. My brother often chose a police show blaring with city sirens and screeching car tires.

Unhappy with this pretend chaos, I'd hug my knees close, stacking dominoes on top of the gray carpet patterned in pink roses. "Let's watch another channel." My words came out in a little-sister whine.

Ken kept his eyes on the screen and said nothing.

I stepped to the television and flipped the manual channel-changer.

Ken, taller and stronger than me, flipped it back. Both of us struggled to wrap our fingers around the plastic knob, twisting it until Mom, who'd been helping with the dishes, noticed.

"You can choose the next show," she told me.

I moved to the kitchen table and traced the red-checked squares with a berry-stained finger. The dishes that Grandma and Mom washed, decorated in red flamingo flowers that looked like Christmas, clinked against the porcelain sink. In the corner, tucked between the fridge and the kitchen counter, was the chair I'd sit in to shake Grandma's fried chicken in a bag just enough to coat it with flour and spices.

Tima, Grandma's cream-colored cat with blue eyes, perched near the stove and watched me. I could pet her if I kept quiet enough. The glass cats on the kitchen shelves were easier to admire. High in the corner, the shiny figures groomed, pounced, and slept, frozen in time, just like Grandma's house.

Grandma came up behind me with a roll of white gauze tape. "Should we name them?"

I nodded yes. Naming the cats would bring them back to life and would also help me forget the test of wills I'd just lost. I took the striped glass kitten she handed me. "Tigger," I said.

Standing on tiptoe in navy-colored Keds, my Grandma, Sarah Bailey Craig, reached up for the next glass cat without protest. When her father Charles quit logging, he moved the family from Elma to Olympia, a city within reach of ocean breezes and the first clouds of Pacific storms. Sarah had three sisters and one brother, Calvin, who died from a shooting accident at age sixteen. A family photo shows Calvin in a pressed suit, forever a young man.

After her first husband, Peter Deisler, died in his mid-forties, Sarah supported her two daughters, my mom and Delores, by working in canneries where salmon, fruit, and other foods were processed. Aged fourteen and ten, the girls pitched in at home and worked jobs once they graduated from high school. Black-and-white photos show a group of women on a road trip, laughing together like three sisters.

My grandma winked at me in the same conspiratorial manner, as if we were in on something. In the years to come, I'd relive her attention to small moments through the letters she wrote to my mom, her descriptions of animals and rain.

"You picked some good names," Grandma said. A half hour later, most of the cats had a taped name sticking onto glass feet. She walked to the stove where my mom boiled water for canning.

I wandered back to the living room where my brother slumped on the gray carpet patterned in roses, still lost in a program's shouts and gunfire. My ears drifted to the kitchen where Mom and Grandma sorted fruit, the feel of steam like warm rain.

Packed in jars and heated on the stove, the berries soon sweetened and turned to jelly. Most jars on the stovetop sealed tight, preserves trapped in time for good eating later on—Mom tapped the jars to make sure. Every so often, a hollow sound revealed an imperfect seal, a restless capture.

"Why don't you two go to the store?" Mom told Ken and me near the end of a weekend at Grandma's. Reading Grandma's copy of *Heidi*, a blue hardcover with Heidi in braids and the Alps in the background, I hadn't yet ventured into an afternoon opaque with clouds. Maybe it was one of those weekends my parents made the four-hour drive southwest of our home to tackle a big project on the 1920s house my grandparents lived in, tiling the bathroom floor or repainting the outer walls.

After years working in Washington and Oregon, Sarah and her second husband, Charles Craig, moved to Ryderwood, Washington, a logging camp turned retirement community. By the time they moved there in the late 1950s, the logging industry had left for more profitable areas, leaving ghost-town rows of houses, a store, and a few other buildings. Aunt Delores told me Grandma hesitated before moving to such an isolated place. Even today, the town perches at the end of the thinnest line a map offers. After a few years, the remoteness of the place, interrupted only by our restless visits, agreed with Grandma.

"It's not supposed to rain," Mom told Ken and me. She was certain about other things, too. Like Ken, she carried the built-in authority of the oldest sibling, leadership sharpened from the early death of her dad. She and her sister Delores agreed on certain memories, from ocean trips to Saturday dances with young soldiers.

Other times, their stories varied. My aunt shared a ghost story about the small house in Olympia where her grandparents, Charles Bailey and Anna Maas Bailey, lived. As small children, Mom, Delores, and a cousin named Charlie explored the dim upstairs rooms. Together, they peered into a closed-off bedroom—a woman sat up in bed. All three kids screamed and fled downstairs to tell the adults, who came upstairs and saw nothing. It was a story I never heard from Mom.

Though the Ryderwood store seemed old and haunted to me—it had a creaky floor and dust layered in years—our errand was more command than suggestion.

Ken shrugged as if he didn't mind getting out of the house. Past Grandma's front yard, his long strides, strengthened from hikes on the mountain where we lived, ate up the sidewalk.

I followed several steps behind. The road beside us stayed quiet and car-free, as if they didn't yet exist. Only the trees shook their leaves against the sky. The space between Ken and me grew. We didn't talk. Instead, I thought about what we'd buy at the store: a Popsicle, candy, maybe both.

An old man, the lines of his face crowding together, watched us from a bench in front of the store. The nearer we came, the more the lines creased. He jutted his chin to Ken without looking at me. "That girl's following you," he said.

Ken glanced at the man and away just as fast, not bothering to correct him.

Inside the dark building, the floor gave away our footsteps in loud squeaks, smells of aged wood and coffee mixing together. With quick steps through the scattered paper and canned goods, we searched for ice cream inside deep cases covered in green-tinged glass. Ken reached for two frostbitten fruit bars and handed one to me. We paid the cashier and scurried back outside, matching steps before Ken's long legs took the lead again.

The man in front of the store, his scowl deepening, watched Ken and me leave. Our disinterest in one another could've been part of some cultural shift he wasn't ready for. During the 1970s, it was just as acceptable to save the trees as to harvest them, easier for youth of any gender to find their own way.

With the distance between us, my brother and I must've seemed more like strangers than siblings to this man. Maybe he was close to his own sister, a fierce memory worth clinging to. He gripped the edges of his chair just as tight. "She's still following you," he bellowed with a hint of anxiety, as if I were an apparition. His voice sounded rough with years and his eyes bored into my brother. "That girl's still behind you."

Not forever, I wanted to say. A few years ago, I'd envied Ken's independence, his walk down our long driveway lined with Douglas fir and cedar so thick they hid the street. My brother's hiking boots crunched on the gravel until he disappeared onto the cul de sac and up the hill where the bus shelter waited. Now, I had my own driveway journey to a later bus on a different route, both of us lurching past the blackberries growing fast as the Pacific Northwest was, almost as fast as we were.

Ken slowed his strides, giving me a rare chance to catch up. He turned and met the man's stare. "She's my sister," he said and kept walking.

The man on the bench nodded and moved his lips, though no words came out. He stared at us hard, as if he didn't buy this less obvious version of family.

Under a white-frosted sky, my own steps lengthened, fortified by a Popsicle and a brother's reluctant claim. Though Ken and I stayed apart, the breeze between us softened, our mismatched steps coming from a similar place.

2

BIGFOOT IN THE BACKYARD

On a hike with Mom up Squak (squawk) Mountain, the foothill we'd moved to on a Halloween night, a branch fell—I jumped. Between dense trees and my own imagination, it was easy to get lost in our backyard, a forest that kept going until it reached the mountaintop. I followed the path and waved a stick to catch spider webs stretching across it. Our lab-collie mix, Buffy, wove under ferns and hopped over the logs Ken threw across the trail to keep out motorbikes, trespassers, maybe even Bigfoot. It made the path harder to find, stumbling through the trees, though Ken said it was just in case.

We walked by huckleberries bursting pink from logs, while evergreens leaned in breezes too tall for me, at eleven years old, to feel. In the damp-smelling air, underbrush crunched again, a squirrel looking for berries. Mom and I created our own share of crackling when our feet lost the trail and stumbled into ferns and purple bleeding hearts. Our jeans turned wet from yesterday's rain.

A few old-growth stumps gave us landmarks and showed the land had once been logged. Just a few years earlier, in 1972, the Bullitt family donated nearly 600 acres at the top of Squak Mountain to the state, under stipulation the land remain preserved. It was the start of an eventual park, the second-growth forest we walked through easing back to wilderness.

At the edge of the second creek, halfway up the mountain, something crashed. The crumpled ferns might've been from a bear; my legs froze, and breathing could wait. Mom stopped in the marshy part of the creek. She wasn't big anyway, at five foot five, and looked smaller listening. I could tell from her eyes she was on the edge of being afraid, if not already there.

It had to be Bigfoot. Sasquatch, his Native American name, matched the sound he made thrashing in the fir trees and smashing ferns. He'd been in the news so much; it had to be. Ken and I read every Bigfoot sighting or report, nevermind that most appeared in the back of the daily newspaper or in feature sections like Northwest Living. We'd pass news stories and pictures of victims, young women in their late teens and twenties with long, straight hair. Their smiles, captured in high school photos, floated across the pages. My stick-straight hair looked a little like theirs. But they were older than me, I'd reason, and lived deeper in Seattle. I saved my worries for Bigfoot.

"Let's go back," Mom said. Her face and voice stayed calm, though the pace she set wasn't. In her raincoat, jeans, and made-for-mud footwear, she turned away from the stream we'd just reached and started running along the trail, the curl in her hair unraveling along the way.

I sprinted behind her, brushing through the ferns and not caring where the raindrops flew. Mom never ran to or from anything. With Buffy tight at her side, she jumped over one of my brother's logs, and I didn't know which to fear more—her boots squelching loud against the trail or the creature behind us. Mom looked back at me once and kept going. Branches cracked from our scrambling, just as noisy as the sounds we ran from. I dropped my spider stick and tore past the webs that grabbed me, not daring to look behind us.

We spotted the bridge over the first creek, the place I thought we'd slow down. Dad built the bridge over the creek with hikes in mind, an invitation to explore the forest rather than run from it. Mom pounded her boots right across it, her small yet solid steps making wood timbers quiver. Past the bridge, she kept running up the hill. At the edge of the woods and in sight of the house, she walked the last few steps, still breathing hard. I stopped, too, and waited for my heart to catch up. The familiar backyard, wild with roses and sweet honeysuckle from Grandma's house, made Sasquatch harder to swallow. Even Buffy, her soft eyes begging for a treat, looked as if she'd forgotten. I pushed the dirt with my sneaker.

Ken, who leaned against the stump where the honeysuckle grew, watched our breathless arrival. Dressed in jeans and a green shirt designed to match the forest, my brother knew deer, bear, and the great-horned owls with their swiveling heads. He stared, not letting us off the hook, waiting in silence to hear why we'd been running.

I looked to Mom, who'd moved away from the trail's end and into the backyard, her favorite place to meander. She was the more credible source in my brother's eyes. After poking some yellow blossoms near a fallen log, she started to weed. "Whatever it was, it was loud." Her words were nonchalant, her attention distant. "Skipper, come here," she said.

With Mom talking to the orange tabby, the story was up to me. My words, too eager, spilled out. "It was big—really big. It crashed through the woods, louder than anything."

Ken, arms crossed in disbelief, slouched deeper against the tree and reacted as he did to all little-sister news. "It was probably a deer." The smirk on his face steadied.

I scowled hard. "No, it was louder."

"A bear, maybe."

Not wanting him to see I was afraid, I stopped talking. Mom, still busy with the dirt, kept just as quiet. I searched her face for clues, a sign we'd fled something worth running from, but the woman who'd raced down the mountain had gone back to the familiarity of the yard, something easier to face than a forest with secrets.

Another mother in the Pacific Northwest fidgeted in front of the sink and watched the coming rain. The worry she wouldn't name was Ted, her son. She'd watched him grow up, first in Pennsylvania and now in the Pacific Northwest. She'd told him she was his sister—because she was unmarried during her pregnancy, it seemed best. Her parents, really his grandparents, became Ted's parents, too. His real father back in Philadelphia was never a part of his life.

When she and Ted moved to Washington, joining distant relatives in Tacoma, her son had a hard time leaving the comfort of his grandparents, though she soon met a man in Tacoma and married. She hoped her son would get along with her new husband. Though the couple did their best to raise Ted, he remained standoffish from his stepfather.

She looked down at the sink and her soapy hands. She never told her son the truth about being his mother. Ever since he'd made a trip back east to meet with the rest of the family, it was as if he knew, though he never discussed it with her.

Now that he was planning to study law, she hoped things would improve. Maybe he'd develop a good career and find a nice girl to marry. Things didn't work out with his first girlfriend, but with his good looks and book smarts, he'd attract someone soon enough.

Like other kids in the 1970s, I was drawn to Bigfoot, and the media responded with plenty of Sasquatch news. Considered a local celebrity, Bigfoot shared coverage with Scotland's Loch Ness Monster and the ominous

Bermuda Triangle in the Atlantic. Adults viewed these mythical accounts as entertainment, something to take their minds off high gas prices and the recession-based risk of losing jobs at major employers like Boeing. For older kids and teenagers like Ken, Bigfoot and Nessie were monsters to whisper about in the dark, unseen creatures more exciting than scary, and precursors to later phenomena like werewolves and zombies.

"There's a Bigfoot movie on TV," Ken told me one night. In the kitchen, he leaned across the beige Formica countertop, his long brown sleeves spanning its width. Mom, plaid fabric all around her, sewed a new shirt in the living room. Dad stayed in the bedroom looking at the work he brought home, airplane diagrams in careful script.

"I'm reading," I said, even though Ken's comment was more command than question. I propped the book I read between my face and the television set, the opening credits already rolling.

"Whatsamatter, you scared?" Even his voice grinned.

"Nooo . . . I've seen those shows already." I didn't want to see the new film clip again, the one where a distinct-looking Bigfoot loped into a clearing before escaping into the screen's fuzzy edges. Although the tape shared no sound, Bigfoot's stride had purposefulness, a determination hard to duplicate. Ken's program could've been a tamer nature show where scientists debated the real and the fake. During one of these specials, a man showed a twenty-inch footprint mold someone had built as a hoax. The fakeness of those prints did nothing to reassure me, not lessening the memory of running through the forest with crashing sounds behind us.

"It's a new movie," Ken said, his eyes already focused on the television. He flicked to the channel he wanted and smiled, probably because he had a chance to watch a movie and scare me at the same time.

I tried to act nonchalant, though television movies were the worst. During the last one I'd seen, a girl sat on a couch watching TV and eating popcorn. At the moment she was happiest, her fuzzy slippers deep in shag carpet, the music grew sinister. From nowhere, Bigfoot thrust a hairy arm through the wood-paneled wall above her head, the girl's screams mixing with spilled popcorn.

My brother turned up the volume and sat in the green chair, the one aimed straight at the TV. From my spot at the kitchen table, I tugged my blue sweatshirt sleeves around my hands and hugged my knees, more willing to face my fear than Ken's scorn. At the opening credits, I debated whether to close the kitchen curtains. With the drapes open, we'd have enough time to spot Bigfoot. Closing them shut out the night and also meant he could sneak up on us. "What about the curtains?" I asked.

Ken's thick eyebrows stayed on the screen. "Don't worry about it." He said it so often to me it was automatic, like others might say *have a nice day*.

I only half-watched the Bigfoot movie. When the music grew dramatic, I stared at the pages of my book. This made-for-TV movie didn't have as much to do with Bigfoot as Ken hoped, though he sat through it anyway. When the ending credits trailed down the screen, I turned away from the television news, unwilling to hear the grim, real-life stories. Before I could run to the fridge, I might catch an update on another slender, straight-haired woman in the Seattle area who'd disappeared, a clean-cut man named Ted, a prime suspect.

A glass filled with Sprite cooled my hand. My brother searched for another show to watch. Mom came into the kitchen to see what we were up to. Even though it was the weekend, I was ready for bed. I walked to my room and pulled on pajamas. Like a turned channel, my thoughts snapped back to Bigfoot. A half hour later and still awake, I listened for Ken in the room next door, a buffer between youthful innocence and what lurked outside.

At dawn, in a home close to the University of Washington shared by several young women, an alarm went off unanswered. Normally, twenty-one-year-old Lynda Healy woke up around 5:30 a.m. to work at a radio station just a few blocks down the street. After work, Lynda studied and spent time with her friends and roommates. One roommate heard the alarm that wouldn't stop. In Lynda's room, finding the bed made up and the room empty, she assumed Lynda had gone to work.

Lynda's family members, who lived on the east side of Lake Washington, came for a dinner Lynda had promised to cook for them that night. Their daughter, who had never arrived at work, didn't show at home. Her parents questioned Lynda's roommates, none of whom had seen her, and called the Seattle police. Their daughter wasn't the type to miss work or class, let alone a family dinner. At first, the police found Lynda's bed made and her room clean, just as her roommate had. Moments later, they determined one of her outfits was missing. They also discovered the bedclothes weren't made up as Lynda would have and a pillow stained with blood.

* * *

I wrestled my sheets and pulled them closer to my chin. Footsteps echoed *thud, thud, thud* on the deck outside my window. My eyes cracked open at the noise. The deck around our house hadn't always reached past my window. Dad added on to the house that summer, wrapping the new deck around the house like gift ribbon. He gave this project every weekend moment until dark-colored boards marched down the house.

"Maybe you could just build it partway," I'd say.

Dad took a break from his nailing. He was tall and lean, with a New England accent revealing itself in certain words to careful listeners. "It'll look better down the whole side," he said. Boards spread out beneath his arms. "Wait and see."

As promised, the new deck blended into the old version as if they were the same. The house, which my dad said had looked like a barn before the deck, gained something from a railing around its midsection, a belt to break it up. No matter how good it looked, I couldn't get used to it. Most nights I lay awake in bed, listening for heavy footsteps on fresh-painted wood. To me, its long timbers were an open invitation to Bigfoot, who'd stomp along its length and stare through the windows.

The thudding sound grew closer. I opened my eyes, just enough to peek through the thin gauze of curtains Mom had made, their pom-pom ball trim bouncing in time to the footprints. In gray light, a shadow passed. It was too slender for Bigfoot, not tall enough. The shadow whistled like a bird—or Dad. The figure turned around and strolled back the way it came.

Burying myself in covers, I rolled away from the window. A new deck meant worse things than Bigfoot. On the edge of adolescence, I sensed other disadvantages, such as curious parents or my brother and his friends peering into my window. I pulled the covers tighter. Other intruders, those I didn't know at all, could just as easily stare inside. Like the stranger named Ted, who some claimed to have appeared at Pickering Barn where I rode horses. I tried to forget the older girls' whispers about this good-looking man, the one who made young women disappear.

Outside of Olympia, my mom's hometown, Donna Manson, a nineteen-year-old attending Evergreen State College, planned to attend a concert. It was springtime, and she'd walk to the event. Donna wasn't seen at the concert or in the days that followed. Her disappearance, in fact, was not initially recorded because of her free-spirited nature and frequent hitch-hiking trips.

During the spring and summer of 1974, several women in their teens and early twenties went missing without a single sign they'd planned to leave, their belongings and clothes found intact at home. Police found little evidence left behind to link anyone to these crimes.

A few witnesses, however, mentioned a man who appeared with his arm in a sling or his leg in a cast. He'd approach a lone woman, someone young and attractive with long, straight hair, and ask her for help carrying his books or packages. The man was polite and clean-cut, charming even. The normality of his mannerisms, a far cry from anything fearsome or mysterious or otherworldly, made him easy to help. No dramatic music accompanied his actions, no random crashing in the trees. Instead, the weather stayed calm, the breeze silent.

On the original part of our deck, Mom read an article from a gardening magazine, sunlight bouncing off its slick pages. She folded her legs beneath the picnic table and stroked Binky, one of our two black cats. Buffy's tail thumped nearby. Although Mom walked on the new deck to gauge the weather, she still read on the old part. I wondered if she was worried about Bigfoot, but it was probably the angle of the sun or the shade of the big cedar that swayed her most.

I made a truce of my own with the new deck. Tearing bits of bread, I placed them on its thin railing for the Steller's jays and smaller chickadees, maybe a western tanager with the male's red head if I were very lucky. In the winter to come, I'd use the new deck to find Orion in the sky and make first footsteps in the snow. I sprawled into a deck chair beside Mom. "What do you think we ran from that day?"

She smiled and shrugged as if I should've forgotten by now. Mom never talked about our run down the mountain. Instead, she saved her concerns for television news, weather reports, and three newspapers stuffed in our mailbox each day, all filled with stories of rain and murder. "Whatever it was, it was probably more scared of us," she said, shifting her chair to gain a little more sun.

While I waited to hear what she thought *it* could've been, a Steller's jay hopped onto the deck rail. His black-bead eyes stared before he snatched the bread and flew to a safer perch, farther from me. I pictured a mother Bigfoot and her child listening in quiet fear to shuffling ferns and crunching sticks, the random noise of humans passing through their forest.

* * *

Twenty-three-year-old Janice Ott, eager to get into the water, hastened her steps to Lake Sammamish State Park, located east of Seattle. The fierce sunshine, rare even in the warmest Pacific Northwest summers, flickered against the lake. Janice lay down her bike, which she'd ridden from her home in downtown Issaquah (ISS a qwah), and settled onto the grass.

On this Sunday afternoon, the park was crowded with people taking advantage of the weather and a day off. One of them, a single man in shorts and a shirt, walked up to Janice. She saw the man with his arm in a sling standing over her, yet couldn't place him—maybe he knew her husband, who was in California temporarily for work.

"Could you help me with my sailboat?" the man asked. He was good looking, with light-brown hair and a slight smile. "I can't load it onto the car with this arm." He pointed toward the parking lot where he'd left his Volkswagen Beetle.

Janice waited before answering. "Sure," she said. "But I don't want to leave my bike."

"You can put it in my car," he said.

Janice picked up her bike and started walking it alongside the man.

He returned the smile and matched her steps. Other witnesses watched the two chatting together on their way to the car.

Janice didn't know this man had already approached other women at the park to ask for help with his sailboat. Before the sun set, there would be not one but two young women missing from what should have been a quiet summer day. Another woman, eighteen-year-old Denise Naslund, would disappear after heading for the park bathrooms later in the afternoon. The sun lengthened its reach. Janice and the man walked farther away from the shining lake and into the trees, closer to the Beetle and darkness.

In the woods behind our house, an overhead branch snapped. I didn't jump. Buffy bounced over a log ahead of me. Mom stayed home on this particular afternoon, reading or working in the yard. Clouds made a ceiling over alders, already bare, while the still-lush Douglas firs waved their branches. Months after our run down the mountain, I didn't mind walking on the path by myself—Bigfoot and I could share. Spider stick in hand, I chose my steps with care and smelled the coming rain.

On a trail thick with ferns and songbirds, it was easier to embrace mythic creatures and ignore realities, like a serial killer who prowled western Washington and later, beyond. The headlines I glossed over in search of Sasquatch news named Ted Bundy, who assaulted several Seattle women during the 1970s. In 1974, he traveled east of the city to the Cascade foothills. Using good looks, charm, and a fake cast, he killed two women at Lake Sammamish, a park below our mountain. Both his victims were young and slim, and both had straight hair. Janice Ott and I shared the same hometown.

Looking up, I touched a gold vine maple leaf, a sign of summer turning to fall. A last grove of bleeding hearts faded nearby. Though I'd made peace with Bigfoot, I wasn't ready for other, more sinister monsters, the everyday kind tougher to spot on walks past streams and huckleberry bushes. I pointed my spider stick a step or two ahead, just enough to see what I knew: the trail, the rain, my brother's logs. Under the sway of Douglas firs, Sasquatch blended softer with the forest and its whispers. Buffy beside me, I scanned the trees and listened.

3
A Palouse Horse

With hoofbeats loud as summer thunder, Moose flew along a mountain trail. His coat, the color of rain clouds, was splashed with black spots. Despite the storm our gallop made, a clear sky arched over this Fourth of July in western Washington. Maple branches, leafy and full, waved at Moose like flags, while the rounded peak of Cougar Mountain, neighbor to Squak Mountain, stretched out behind us. Lengthening his stride, the horse created his own breeze and ignored me, the skinny teenager on his back.

I pulled both reins at once, a mistake; Moose was too powerful. I didn't know yet to pull back on one rein or to lean back until my weight eased his strides. An hour earlier, I'd borrowed Moose from the local stable for a ride on the trails. On days off from my summer job working as a server for a twenty-four-hour restaurant, I tacked up a horse and headed for the hidden paths on Cougar Mountain. Like my home on nearby Squak Mountain, Cougar was filled with small streams, deer, maybe a bear. A few signs of civilization lingered, from the mines dotting the landscape to a hermit who lived on the mountaintop. I carried a whip, not for the mountain man or Moose, but for loose dogs on the road below that might spook a horse.

Moose, a better horse than I was a rider, took care of himself. I watched his ears swivel, as if he were surprised I was still there. His eye rolled back at me and looked away just as fast. I tightened my legs and ducked my head beneath the branches. Though I'd spent hours grooming horses to strengthen my arms and weeks circling the arena to improve my balance, I still needed more time in the saddle to perfect my seat. Going fast seemed a quicker way to get there, but it was a strategy that'd gotten me in trouble, turning this ride through the foothills into something inevitable, a journey as tumultuous as Moose's own history.

* * *

Appaloosas, known for their speed, stealth, and spots, were first bred extensively in North America by the Nez Perce of eastern Washington and Idaho. White Americans in the area named this horse for the Palouse River where several Nez Perce peoples lived, calling the breed "A Palouse Horse." This term later became one word, "Appaloosa."

Some historians believe the Nez Perce bred and trained Appaloosa horses from stock that escaped or was stolen from the conquistadors, who explored North America in the sixteenth century. Others say the horses came from the Shoshones of southern Idaho and Native American tribes of the Great Plains, while still others suggest the horses crossed the land bridge many years ago.

Under the care of the Nez Perce, who practiced selectivity by either castrating horses not used for breeding or giving away less valuable animals, the Appaloosa thrived. In addition to careful breeding, the combination of mountain grasses in the summer and sheltered valleys in the winter benefited the horses. Soon, the spotted herds spread across the rugged grasslands. The striking Appaloosa contributed to the Nez Perce reputation for horsemanship and helped their people become wealthy.

The Appaloosa Museum in Moscow, Idaho, relates how the horses changed the Nez Perce way of life in other important ways. Some Nez Perce stayed closer to fishing villages, and others adopted a mobile horse culture. The non-horse peoples adapted more easily to the white European's vision of individual property. The independence and far-reaching realms of Nez Perce horsemen, meanwhile, conflicted with the white settlers' hopes for land, leading to growing dissent in what is now the intersection of Washington, Oregon, and Idaho.

Moose leaned against the reins and picked up speed. His legs blurred. My own legs ached, and I wasn't sure how to get out of this. I tried to tell myself there was a reason for this wild gallop, though what it might have been was swallowed up in hoofbeats. Maybe Moose was tired of his stall with a short paddock in the back and arena rides that went nowhere. Maybe he needed this mountain run, this release from everyday confines, just as much as I did.

I started riding when I was fourteen, and Mom took me to lessons. Once I had a learner's permit to drive, I borrowed the green station wagon and drove to the barn myself, financing lessons by cleaning stalls and helping out at feed time. My parents listened to me talk about the barn with patient unease—their own histories didn't include horses.

Mom, who came from a family rooted in logging and homesteading, thought horses were big, utilitarian, and dangerous. Though she drove me willingly to riding lessons, she rarely watched, dreading falls that were sure to come. For Dad, it was the social class that bothered him most. Near his parents' house in rural Massachusetts, he watched hunt club riders canter across the fields in trim coats. This scene represented a foreign country to him, one he wasn't sure he wanted me stepping into. Despite their view of horses, I was determined to ride in my own way. I rode English, the same style as riders in the hunt club, though I made do with an oversized, second-hand saddle and borrowed horses instead of having my own. Rather than riding in a private pasture, I spent hours strengthening my legs and practicing my balance in the mountain foothills.

The forest whirred by, scarier than scenic. Moose, who was both young and fit, swallowed the ground in gulps. We left the trees and slipped into the lowlands on the other side of Cougar Mountain. I kept Moose on the trail as best I could, unwilling to fall into a coal mine shaft or run smack into the white-bearded mountain man, the one who shook his index finger at stray riders and told them to get off his land. The grasslands spread before us, empty of development for the time being. Once we hit the lowlands, similar to eastern Washington slopes where Moose's Appaloosa cousins ran, my chances of stopping him would be even less.

Sunlight dappled the ground like water. I dropped the reins along with a handful of white mane. Moose didn't notice. I drifted off his left side, slipping in slow motion. I floated for what seemed like minutes between blue skies and pounding hooves. A second or two later, I traded midair flight for packed dirt. There was no splash when I hit, just scattered leaves when the hard path met my side. No water filled my mouth, just a gasp of air when I realized I was okay. I stood up quickly to shake off dirt and stray fears. I took a step and reached out for the white streak that was Moose—any hopes of stopping him disappeared in waves of dust. He galloped on, reins flapping against the empty saddle, until his last spots faded from sight.

In June of 1877, a herd of horses, many of them Appaloosas, fanned across the plains of the Camas Prairie in what is now Idaho, their spots making shadows against the grasslands. They belonged to the last Nez Perce not living on reservations. Growing unrest over their land and horses had convinced several leaders to relocate in Idaho, to US lands set aside for them in Lapwai. Travel to this reservation included difficult rivers, the Snake and the Salmon. Still, the Nez Perce knew the terrain and their horses were fit.

One of the young warriors, Wahlitits, paraded the camp on horseback with the other young men until his horse stepped on a woman's blanket by mistake. Researcher Kent Nerburn tells of Yellow Grizzly Bear's scathing words, which chastised Wahlitits for making camp rounds rather than avenging his father's slow death at the hand of a settler. Wahlitits struggled for the rest of the evening, torn between the word he'd given his father not to seek revenge and a desire for action in the midst of this forced journey. Later that night, he and his cousins gathered their horses and slipped outside the sleeping encampment. The skirmishes they planned were quick; their targets specific. Among the dead was Samuel Benedict, ancestor of my dad's neighbor in western Washington.

The Nez Perce encampment awoke to news of the night's battles, with rumors of US soldiers on the way. Although most of the gathered Nez Perce, which included elders, women, and children, did not want war, they were now forced to save themselves. Led by their tribal chiefs, with several thousand of their most carefully bred horses, the Nez Perce were on the run.

I walked the way I'd come, this time without Moose. The noon sun weighed heavy with no shadows to hide what happened. Although flying along these paths took seconds, returning would take at least an hour. I didn't worry about the mountain man, loose dogs, or wildlife along the way. I thought about Moose, and the path he'd take without me. Years ago, our pasts were even more conflicting, though our most recent history came closer to mind.

The first time I met Moose, a horse trainer named Nancy unsaddled him, slid the bridle off his head, and set him free to walk down the barn aisle. I reached my hand out, a helpless movement to direct this horse that needed no guidance. He strode into his stall to grab a mouthful of hay, ears pinned back as a warning.

Nancy motioned for me to let him be. "That's Moose," she said, as if this explained everything.

I nodded and watched him eat. Unlike me, Moose was graceful and self-assured. I was sixteen, with a face full of braces and metallic-rimmed glasses. Moose was a leopard Appaloosa, with dramatic black spots against an all-white body, the pattern used by experienced riders to blend with the trees when hunting or at war. I'd seen plenty of these horses in western Washington, from the full-body spotted varieties like Moose to the horses with white blankets and spots only on their hindquarters. I knew they were horses of the Nez Perce, who bred them across the mountains in eastern Washington. I didn't know many specifics of the Nez Perce, let alone my own history in the area, our tangled heritage a distant cloud.

Nancy nodded at Moose, who rolled his eye at us. "You'll ride him in the lesson."

Unsure what to expect, I listened to the trainer but gazed at the horse. A few days later, I returned wearing jeans and cheap rubber riding boots, enough to get by. The minute I slipped onto Moose's back, he ambled to the middle of the arena. I rebalanced in the oversized saddle and directed him back to the rail. At the trot, a two-beat gait between a walk and canter, Moose skirted the corners, making our route more oblong than rectangular.

Nancy watched me from along the fence rail. "Try a canter," she said.

Moose was eager, too eager, to break into this faster, three-beat gait. I tried to aim him deeper into the corners. Instead, we headed for the railing. His ears pricked like tiny radars. I'm not sure whether Moose misunderstood my aids or was bored by my lack of direction. Either way, the result was the same. He sailed over the three-foot arena fence, which opened into pasture, while I stayed on his back with clamped legs and a handful of mane. Moose tore thick mouthfuls of grass afterwards as if nothing had happened. Nancy saw we were all right and laughed.

After my slow walk down the mountain, I saw the pasture where Moose jumped the fence during our first ride, the same pasture where I hoped he'd be. At first glance, he wasn't in sight, and neither was Nancy. I opened the gate and crossed the pasture to make sure. Maybe someone else had seen Moose arrive, tired but unharmed, and put him in his stall. Inside the barn, horses snorted and flitted their ears; all of them except Moose. My feet were sore, my mouth dry. Other than the soft movements the horses made, the stable was quiet, other riders having stowed their tack and gone home to Fourth of July picnics. I swallowed hard and picked up the phone to call Nancy. My voice cracked into the receiver. No decent rider would lose her horse. "Moose is on Cougar Mountain," I said. "I fell off, and he's gone."

* * *

Draped in darkness, spotted horses grazed at the Big Hole campsite. After brief skirmishes with white soldiers sent to capture them, the Nez Perce moved into territory they knew well, the Bitterroot Mountains of what is now Idaho and Montana. Nez Perce leaders breathed easier, assuming the soldiers had given up. At this campsite along a river, they saw an opportunity to regroup, to give their livestock a rest. Chief Joseph, who managed the campsites, made sure the women and children were settled and the valuable horse herd safe. After the last campfire faded into night, a lone Nez Perce glided between the horses, which dozed in warm breaths.

Several warriors dreamed of a battle that night. Wahlitits, the warrior whose actions helped spur the Nez Perce into flight, envisioned his own death. His premonition was as close as the white soldiers camping nearby. Colonel Gibbon, a soldier charged with the Montana territory, planned a surprise attack on the Nez Perce. Gibbon and his men were the ones surprised, however, by a man slipping among the horses to check on them. A shot rang out as soldiers charged the camp.

When a bullet from one of the soldiers struck and killed Wahlitits, his wife grabbed a rifle and kept shooting until she, too, was struck and killed. Both sides faced losses, among them Nez Perce women and children. The Nez Perce covered their dead, packed their belongings, and fled the camp before the army could attack again.

Moving faster than before, the Nez Perce shifted east through Yellowstone and north toward Montana, outrunning both the soldiers and the first snows of autumn. The longer the journey stretched over the summer, the more people died of exhaustion—some of the elders asked to be left behind rather than continue. The Nez Perce were also forced to leave behind lame and exhausted horses along the way. Joseph, in his role as camp leader, spoke against the continued flight and suffering, which had stretched to three months.

After weeks of swift travel, the Canadian border, which marked the end of the Nez Perce journey, was a day's ride away. Not only did Canada mean freedom from the United States but also possible aid from allies, the Sioux. Just forty miles, a short distance compared to the miles the Nez Perce had traveled; freedom waited at the border. Close as Canada was, the distance proved too great. US soldiers attacked the Nez Perce, killing several of their leaders. The remaining Nez Perce, under cover of a hillside barricade, managed to hold off their enemies. Over the next few days, both sides waited in a standoff—the Nez Perce for Sitting Bull and the Sioux; the soldiers, for supplies. Six days later, the soldier's reinforcements arrived first.

Chief Joseph met with the remaining tribal leaders. They'd come within sight of a new country, but from their cold shelter in the hill, it wasn't close enough. Many wanted to stay and fight. A few others planned an escape to Canada by nightfall. Joseph, responsible for four hundred Nez Perce and a thousand of their horses, knew many of the people could go no further. He addressed the chiefs once more. *Hear me, my chiefs. I am tired. My heart is sick and sad. From where the sun now stands, I will fight no more forever.*

The fireworks my brother and I bought at the closest reservation sparked overhead like usual but held no joy. With every pop and crackle of the cones and sparklers, my mind was on the mountain with Moose. It was the worst Fourth of July celebration of my life, filled with anything but freedom.

In October 1877, General Sherman exiled the Nez Perce to Indian Territory in Oklahoma—their remaining horses were sold, shot by soldiers, or taken by white settlers. The US government, fearful the Nez Perce might once again use their horses for war, ordered breeding of adopted Appaloosas to draft horses in an attempt to dilute their grace and swiftness. Seven difficult years later, the Nez Perce were allowed to return to reservations in Idaho and Washington. Joseph ended his days at a reservation in the northern part of Washington, returning to the region in 1884, but never to his original home.

Other than appearances in western shows and circus acts, the Nez Perce spotted horses fell under the radar until 1937, when an article in *Western Horseman* rekindled interest. The Appaloosa was established as a breed in 1938. Despite earlier efforts to minimize these horses, their strength and savvy persisted.

A day and a half later, my friends at the barn found Moose on the mountain. Having a saddle in place for several days had swollen the area where the girth circled his belly, but otherwise, he was in good health. I fed him as many carrots as I could stuff in my pocket. He lipped them, yet kept a careful eye on me. In days to come, I'd learn to ride in the arena and over fences, practicing with Moose until we were good enough to compete in local shows and come home with a ribbon or two.

East of the mountains, the Nez Perce and Appaloosa continue their partnership through the Nez Perce Horse Registry, started at the reservation in Lapwai, Idaho, in 1995. In conjunction with the Nez Perce Young Horsemen Project, which teaches youth ages fourteen to twenty-one about horsemanship, the registry strengthens original qualities prized by the Nez Perce, from intelligence and distinctive markings to agility and swiftness.

I found Moose again, years later, at the local racetrack. Working as a lead pony, he guided high-strung racehorses to the starting gate. This job, requiring a combination of steadiness and speed, suited Moose. His walk was assured, his coat dry compared to the nervous thoroughbred beside him. From a trot, Moose eased into a four-beat gallop, inching ahead of the racehorse to show him how it was done. I pressed against the railing, closer to fanning manes and flying dirt. Still in the lead, Moose's eye turned to mine, our past rekindled in a stride before he galloped on by.

4

After the Volcano

We flew by Mount St. Helens and watched the mountain spit smoke plumes. It was murmuring again, repeating warnings from twenty years before. Spirit Lake, buried in the 1980 eruption, belonged to the dead, according to Native American legend. The mountain might not be finished reclaiming sacred ground. From a commercial jet, not too close, I strained to glimpse its ragged and powerful edges. I remembered the time before, engrossed in my own life as a teenager, not noticing the slow shifts in my surroundings. Back then, I'd doubted the volcano.

A postcard mountain in the Cascade Range, Mount St. Helens looked too serene to be a volcano. It curved upward like a replica of Mount Fuji, perfect in its inverted, ice-cream cone shape. About 100 miles south of our home, apart from neighboring peaks, the mountain stood alone in white calm. Volcanoes were the stuff of exotic places, like Hawaii and Pompeii. Natural disasters did not happen in Washington State. No tornadoes, no loud thunderstorms, floods a rarity despite all the moisture. The only emergency drill we had in school was for earthquakes, hiding under our desks yet sure nothing would happen.

The murmurs from Mount St. Helens, which began on March 20, had that same vagueness. It was a familiar oddity, nothing to get excited about. Geologists gave updates on these rumblings so often that they became ordinary, like rain reports. It was something for adults to care about, like income taxes and the weather. While the mountain stirred, my teenage attention focused on horses. Their gentle power and sweet hay breath drew me from the structure of classes, the rules of home. When school let out during late spring afternoons, I borrowed the green station wagon and drove to May Valley Stable about two miles from my house. I cleaned stalls and helped with the evening feed, earning rides on the scary-smart Moose. I galloped alone on nearby Cougar Mountain, staying on the trails to avoid the mines and the mountain man, his beard thick as underbrush.

"Say you're lost," a friend at the barn advised me about encounters with this man who'd claimed the mountaintop. I only saw him once on my own. Though he didn't speak, his frown asked me what I was doing there. "I'm finding my way back," I said, my words too quick. The mountain man murmured under his breath, as if resigned to the presence of visitors like me. He turned in the other direction, back to the realm he'd taken for his own.

Harry Truman, the man with a presidential name and an imposing outlook to match, didn't let mountain rumblings bother him. The eighty-three-year-old managed a lodge on Mount St. Helens, his home for the past fifty years. Having outlived his third wife, he remained at Spirit Lake with sixteen cats for company and a pink '57 Cadillac for fun. His past included hunting, flying planes, and bootlegging booze from Canada. In Truman's backyard, Mount St. Helens shook with small tremors. Like a fresh bruise, the pressure from within bulged against the mountain's northern face.

Truman attracted attention not for his life on the mountain, but because of his refusal to leave it. While I plotted horseback getaways, Truman fought to stay. He became a Mount St. Helens's mascot to both local and national media. Rather than becoming annoyed with the attention of mountain visitors, Truman gave frequent interviews about why he chose to stay on the mountain despite geologists' warnings. As the legend of Truman grew, it became more difficult for him to leave both home and proud words behind, myth and man entangled in the lakeside setting. Truman was not alone in his desire to remain on the mountain. Other property owners who also wanted to stay grew restless with the geologists' warnings, particularly given the quiet that spilled over Mount St. Helens in early May. A few of them pointed out that in Hawaii, you could drive right up to the lava flows.

From the news reports I watched over dinner, I decided that Truman and his cats would be all right. Just like our weather reporters who tried in vain to find sunny days, the geologists too would be wrong. Some of them predicted a large, sudden blast. Others favored a gentle eruption, something you could tour. No one thought it was a good idea for Truman to remain so close to the mountain summit, but he refused to form an escape plan. Although the point of science was to know things, none of the experts knew what the mountain would do, what Truman would do.

Given my own restlessness, I didn't understand his steadfastness.

"Do you think he'll come down?" I asked Ken.

"If he were smart he would."

"So, you think something's going to happen?

"I dunno. Maybe."

My brother, the meteorology student in college, didn't know better than anyone else. It remained an issue for others to solve, something that didn't concern me. I shrugged and went back to my room, thinking about which horse I'd ride the next day, whether Moose or the bay thoroughbred named Oliver Twist.

On Sunday, May 18, I drove to the stable in the morning, determined to spend as much of the day riding as possible. The crabgrass reached for the sun, clouds parted to open sky. I cleaned stalls, rode Oliver over a few jumps, and put away the tack, old leather smell mixing with the leg liniment. I even wrapped the gelding's black legs in support bandages, just in case, while his muzzle explored the waiting oats. When I couldn't find any more excuses to stay, mane to untangle, or bits of straw to sweep, I drove back home late that afternoon.

My parents and brother stood in the kitchen watching television when I arrived. Their attention didn't budge as the picture flickered. I watched their folded arms and grim expressions and wondered what had happened to keep them inside—Mom didn't waste sunny days. No one commented on my hours away from home, another surprise.

"The mountain blew," my brother said, his face still aimed at the television.

I didn't know if he was teasing, but Mom nodded agreement.

"Dad heard it first thing," she said. Her own eyes didn't waver from the screen, unusual for her.

I replayed my version of the morning. The only loud sounds I'd heard were horseshoes clicking on concrete, the thump of my feet finding ground when I jumped off a horse's back, a plane overhead buzzing into the clouds. A volcano had exploded somewhere between the hooves and sky, and I had missed it.

The television announcer's voiced droned. "For those of you who are just now tuning in, Mount St. Helens erupted at around 8:30 this morning, surpassing even expert predictions of what this active volcano might do. Since early March, scientists have been carefully monitoring seismic activity associated with the mountain . . ."

The images showed a raging mountain in black and white. Time-lapse photos depicted a blast that imploded in dense clouds of smoke and ash. Rather than erupting upward as predicted, the explosion burst sideways from the mountain, a mushroom cloud of smoke hovering in the final images.

The station switched from the photo series to live footage of the Toutle River, which flowed at the base of Mount St. Helens. The once calm water now gorged on mud, logs, and one house roof. It looked like the floods in the South after thunderstorms, or one of the East Coast hurricane scenes. The station must have had only one piece of river footage, because it showed the same roof scene over and over. Yet another station followed the structure as it approached a bridge. We cringed as the roof came closer to the cement supports and crumbled to kindling against them. I turned away from the television, not wanting to see more.

"What about Harry?" I asked. Dad said nothing, just looked hard at the screen.

More than fifty people died in the blast of Mount St. Helens, Harry Truman among them. With twenty-four megatons of thermal energy, the mountain's northern face blew off in the direction of Spirit Lake. Native American legend came true—the area belonged to the dead. As Truman's lodge was located about four miles from the mountain summit, the lateral blast took about ninety seconds to reach him. Within a minute and a half, several hundred feet of mud covered his lodge and lake. Truman had little more than a few seconds to glance in surprise from his morning coffee and then recognize the event for what it was. Although some speculated that Truman had planned to leave once he saw the lava flow, he never had a chance. He stayed with his mountain, as promised. Twin spirits, Harry and his lake, shared their demise.

Two others lost in the immediate blast zone, geologist David Johnston and news photographer Reid Blackburn, had followed the mountain since its early rumblings. Johnston, the young bearded geologist, left his final words on a radio transmission, "Vancouver, Vancouver, this is it." The excitement of the event reached him before the doom of the blast hit. Even in death, the eruption to Johnston was about discovery, not self.

Further down the mountain, twelve miles from the summit, a family of four perished in a Chevy Blazer. In the same campground area, eight people died trying to escape the violent mudflows. Several loggers, there for work, also died. The mud captured some mid-sentence, preserving them in poses that looked like picture taking. I hoped they never knew what hit them, preferring to remember them snapping their cameras in awe.

Animals also lost their lives on the mountain, including 7,000 deer, elk, and bear. Countless birds and small mammals died from the blast. In the rivers, 40,000 young salmon were killed from the choking mud and fallen trees. In towns like Castle Rock at the foot of the mountain, some residents claimed to see fish trying to jump out of the hot waters. Their escape made my teenage flights to the stable seem trivial. I thought of those desperate fish and envisioned a net, large as the sky, to save them.

Along with ground devastation, scientists kept their eyes on the horizon, anxious to see where the three mile-wide ash cloud would spread. It had already drifted 80,000 feet upward from its mountain origins. I ran outside the house to search for ash. Having missed the blast, I could at least share the volcanic aftermath and feel as if I'd experienced an event. I peered south where the mountain lay, but the sky looked clear as before, the late afternoon sun unfailing. Only some dense clouds hinted at volcanic forces; it was hard to tell them apart from the usual rain clouds.

Meanwhile, three miles of ash, enough to fill a football field 150-feet deep, floated eastward after the lateral blast. The prevailing winds pushed it across the Cascades until it snowed down in thick layers over eastern Washington. I watched the haunted scenes on television of darkened skies in midday, people in masks, cars with their headlights on. I wanted to be in those towns where the dust fooled the streetlight sensors, turning on the lights in Yakima, Ritzville, and Spokane. But I was west of the mountain, and safe.

I imagined myself into the science fiction scenes the television showed us, envious of the gray snow. In southeastern Washington, several inches of ash fell. Traces of it traveled beyond the state, as far eastward as North Dakota and southwest to Colorado. A random portion of ash found its way to Oklahoma, settling into an oval-shaped region. It didn't stop in the United States, but continued eastward, circling the globe in less than three weeks. The ash fall of this altered landscape danced around me, skirting a high school life filled with student newspaper deadlines and horses, a blanket I never felt.

Even my parents experienced its effects more fully, their annual Memorial Day trip to decorate gravestones in Olympia coated with ash and rain on the way there. The cars coming from the south, Dad told me, were smeared with mud. I pictured my parents driving through the snow-like substance and leaving the cemetery hours earlier than usual, ash following them home.

After the ash settled and the horizon came back into view, the main problem was what to do with it. Entrepreneurs from the eastern half of the state did not wait long to scoop it up and transform the breaths of dust into finery. Mount St. Helens's ash took many shapes, from sculptures and shot glasses to magnets, coffee mugs, and pumice soap.

On a trip to downtown Seattle with Mom, I bought a few Mount St. Helens's ash Christmas ornaments spotted in an outdoor stall at Pike Place Market, right between the vegetables and cultivated honey. I still had only experienced the volcano with the indifference of distance and youth. I might as well have been from New York; my involvement had been so little. These new ash figures, fired from volcanic rock, minerals, and glass, gave me a small, albeit trivial, part. The souvenirs and I, token players, remained peripheral to the event itself, a reporter from the outside looking in.

During a clear summer day two years later, perfect for weekend horseback riding, Dad suggested we make the two-and-a-half hour trip south to Mount St. Helens. Because the mountain had cooled, the danger wasn't as great. Although he didn't say it, I also knew he wanted us to see the mountain on our own terms, free of television commentary and replayed footage. But I'd long since given up participating in the mountain tragedy.

"I'll go," Mom said. In the laundry room closet, she started looking for the right shoes, something between hiking boots and sneakers. She didn't pressure me, probably realizing I'd dig in my teenage heels.

Dad dug through the hall closet for binoculars, taking down the basket of flashlights and batteries from the top shelf. Like Mom, he didn't offer an opinion on whether I should go.

In the midst of their preparation, I hesitated, missing my brother's eye for landscape and weather. "Is Ken going?" I asked.

"No, he's busy with school."

I waited another minute or so and then set aside my riding boots and joined Mom on the hunt for tough hiking shoes. Here was an opportunity to make amends for what I'd missed as an outsider to the event, a teenager lost on that wide expanse between self and remote concerns. I could always go riding another day. Two years after the fact, I had a chance to meet the mountain, witnessing its transformation firsthand.

The three of us drove along I-5, the highway signs guiding us south toward the Oregon border. I watched the Aberdeen exit go by, our usual vacation route for ocean weekends. Nothing seemed different along the way, trees filing alongside the car and a few clouds floating.

We aimed for the Toledo exit, the same route to the house where my grandparents had lived. Dad drove past Toledo on a road that grew more remote and sparse before ending at the foot of Mount St. Helens. It was midmorning, and we were the only tourists wandering through volcano country. The landscape stood dry and alone, parched gray from ash fall.

The road ended near a former Weyerhaeuser logging station. We left the car and crossed what used to be a green meadow by foot, heading for the closest knoll. The wind gusted by in tufts, with little vegetation to break it. Dust swirled up and made me sneeze, a gritty feel I forgot once Mount St. Helens came into full view. The uneven ice-cream cone mountain startled me. Its former science-fair symmetry now looked jagged, primeval. Nothing stood between it and our binoculars; no trees or hillside softened its threat.

We wandered back to the car and drove along the Toutle River, following its path downstream from the mountain. Although the water had long since returned to a normal flow and was no longer brown with mud, we could still see the inland gouges where it had scoured new boundaries into the banks. Remembering images of the Toutle choked with trees and the roof that had smashed into a bridge, I thought of those who'd experienced the river's fury firsthand. While I'd had a television between tragedy and me, they'd had none.

We drove back to a sign that offered chartered flights on the outskirts of the town. "How would you like to fly over the mountain?" Dad asked.

"I'll do it," I said without waiting to decide. I waved to Mom, who opted to stay behind, a view of the mountain from the ground enough for her. With nervous energy I climbed into a seat behind Dad and the pilot, who guided the humming plane into the smooth and windless sky.

Once he reached the mountainside, the pilot curved in an arc around Mount St. Helens, which waited for us like a piece of the moon, rocky and dark. The airplane engine sounded small and thin against the backdrop. We saw flattened trees, toothpick-sized, by the thousands. They lay where they'd fallen, blasted in one direction by the volcano. The pilot told us that loggers were still cutting them into pieces in preparation for eventual harvest.

"Look at the ponds," Dad said.

He pointed to craters of water, orange and green from volcanic chemicals. Maybe this was how the world had started, bare and fiery. Even a few years later, nothing grew on the ash turf surrounding these pools.

The pilot motioned us to look where Spirit Lake had once been, its contours filled with silt and logs.

"Truman's old home," I mumbled to no one. I admired his conviction, even though it led to his death. He'd settled for nothing less than full participation, refusing to look on from a distance.

The plane bounced as we came closer to the crater's edge. The pilot steered us near the rim, but was careful not to cross it.

"Does the heat cause this turbulence?" Dad said. Whether through his work as an engineer for Boeing or curiosity in general, he looked more interested than alarmed.

The pilot nodded, circling the mountain but never crossing the summit lest we hurtle out of control, into the volcano rather than around it. Even on the outskirts, the plane shook. I gripped the seat to keep my stomach still. Although we didn't cross the volcano mouth, our path wavered near enough to look down into it, open and deep. I watched it spit thin towers of steam, warning us.

Once the plane landed, we walked to Mom in the car in satisfied quiet, having met the mountain in its backyard. I felt closer to what had happened, no longer a bystander taking quick glances from the safer boundaries of my own world. Just as I was becoming more aware of events around me, the mountain too was changing. Geologists predicted vegetation and animal life would one day cover the mountain. Playing devil's advocate, they cautioned in the same breath the mountain would erupt again no matter how quiet it might appear, geology restless as the West.

From our drive on the interstate, Mount St. Helens disappeared from sight yet still followed me home. After the volcano, things beyond the immediate mattered, and being part of a place meant more than just living there. The mountain, whose early whispers I'd disbelieved, took lives and swept forest contours into a lunar landscape. In years to come, flying over Mount St. Helens on trips from my own shifting surroundings, I'd study its flattened top line with humility. Nestled in the Cascades, the broken Mount Fuji looked serene in its deceptive quiet and wisps of cloud. Although the snow softened it, the volcano, silent for now, waited.

5
Three Stages of Sustenance

Efficiency

On the eastern side of Snoqualmie Pass, we left the Cascade Mountains and rain clouds further behind us. My friend Nicole and I traveled on I-90 in a two-seater convertible, the tiny car humming across the pass splitting Washington State in two. Bound for Pullman and site of the university Nicole attended, we traveled deeper into a fertile landscape on the other side of the state.

The view east of the Cascades defied the rainy Northwest stereotype most imagined, with pines rather than Douglas fir and colors more pink and gold than green. Within easy reach of the sun, an interior climate nurtured apples and cherries, peaches and apricots, and in the state's southeastern corner, wheat fields and college students.

The day turned warm, the wind fanning scarves Nicole and I wore. I used to think I'd be happy staying close to home and working in the western part of the state, not considering what a different landscape might yield. Two years past the drift of Mount St. Helens's volcanic ash, which blew eastward in 1980, I started my own inland trek in search of a different view.

"Do you like it here?" I hollered at Nicole over the road noise. I couldn't see her eyes—sunglasses protected our features from more persistent daylight than we were used to.

Her blonde, short hair barely contained by its scarf, Nicole nodded above the noise, leaving me to wonder if it was the school, the fact she kept a horse nearby, or the chance to be four and a half hours away from home. Her answer, no matter the motive, rang true. As a communications student in a busy downtown campus, I could see the benefit of a change of scenery, a new vantage point to shape one's life.

Miles after crossing the Columbia River, the terrain altered even more. Grain elevators sprouted instead of trees, surrounded by wheat fields and towns with names like Washtucna and Dusty. Outside one of these small communities, someone had scrawled Washington State University's "WSU" acronym on a railroad trestle, like a milestone.

As a teenager, I'd stood on a ladder picking cherries too taut for their own skins, on the verge of bursting. My parents and I had traveled from the western side of the mountains to the Yakima Valley and the small town of Selah, the sky clear after days of gray. I balanced a box of fruit against the tree and tried not to lean too far into branches so thick they looked as if they'd catch me.

Nicknamed "the fruit bowl of the nation," the Yakima Valley region employed farmers, full-time workers, and migrant and seasonal farm workers to meet agricultural demands. The Farm Workers in Washington State History Project describes the varied ethnic makeup of those working in the fields, from Native Americans and white Americans to immigrants from Europe, Asia, and Latin American.

While fruit production dominated the Yakima Valley, wheat flourished in the southeastern corner of the state. A 1938 photo shows a Rumley combine pulled by thirty-two horses and guided by five men. Taken in Whitman County, the photographer captured the horses headfirst and knee deep in wheat, just-plowed rows beside them. Mechanized harvesters built to manage these slopes, which slanted as steep as fifty percent, would soon replace these teams. The result yielded additional crops yet burdened the landscape with depleted soil and erosion. The horses, meanwhile, were reassigned as pleasure mounts in smooth-sided terrain.

On our way to a summertime riding clinic, Nicole and I made good time, traveling deeper into the state than I'd ever been. The hills of the Palouse country appeared first, dune-like and covered in wheat rather than sand. Formed by lava plateaus from the last ice age, the slopes rolled all the way to the horizon, a geographic feature matched in few other places. WSU and the city of Pullman perched on the nearest hills, forming a college town oasis in Whitman County. Similar to the desert, the region received as little as eleven inches a year depending on which way the hill sloped.

Despite the lack of rain and soil prone to erosion and drifting, the rich loess nurtured winter wheat, light-colored crops waving in sunlit unison. Prior to modern farming methods, soil loss made an even bigger impact, with the US Department of Agriculture mapping soil losses between fifteen to eighteen tons per acre per year in the heavily farmed region of the Palouse River basin from 1939 to 1972. Between intensive farming practices, an absence of native prairie grasses, and prevailing winds, the soil wasn't easy to keep in place. The 25,000 college students descending on the city of Pullman, population 6,500, proved just as restless.

Nicole showed me her college dorm room, an ample space compared to the narrow triple bunk I slept in at the University of Washington in Seattle. Nicole's room, which she shared with a roommate, offered a mirror view of two desks, two beds, and two bedside shelves for books, along with one mini-fridge beneath the window. Outside, the landscape billowed in wheat.

In the latter part of the twentieth century, farming practices promoting a longer-term view joined advances in production and mechanization. During a 1970s wave of organic farming, researchers looked for ways to achieve yields while enriching and preserving the land. A WSU Extension fact sheet describes three stages of sustainability—efficiency, alternatives, and redesign—to improve existing farm processes. An efficient farm might rotate multiple crops, similar to the fruit-picking farms I visited with my parents, or pattern their crops in new ways to ensure soil health paired with a high yield.

After the dorm tour, Nicole drove me to the stable where she kept her horse, a newer facility with an indoor riding arena. We watched a riding lesson in progress, the way the instructor shaped the rider into a more effective posture. On the way back to Pullman, we stopped at a second barn closer to campus. This particular stable offered a simple layout with indoor stalls and outdoor runs for each horse, a no-nonsense design. People rode English and western-style and shared an outdoor arena year-round in a small but practical space. I pictured my horse in the weathered barn with a paddock of his own, the hills we'd ride on rippling in the background.

Alternatives

I want to transfer schools, I told my parents after the trip to Pullman. It wasn't just the landscape luring me—the Communications Department at WSU had offered me a journalism scholarship and the possibility of working for the student newspaper, a paid writing position. Just as enticing was the idea of living on my own again, even at a distance from what I knew.

I'd started as a freshman at the University of Washington in Seattle, the most urban place I'd ever lived. My friend Anne, who also rode horses, had joined a sorority there, and I pledged the same one, not anticipating the very order I'd wanted to escape, with rules about studying and what to wear. I struggled with my new living situation more than the schoolwork.

One morning, I discovered a homeless woman huddled in a storage area of the basement to keep warm—she'd made a refuge where I found none. I thought about reaching out to her, but one of the house members asked her to leave. I was naive in other ways, thinking nothing of walking home at night by myself on the same streets Ted Bundy had killed a young woman.

The most memorable part of living in the big house was escaping it with Anne. We'd sign out for dinner, leaving social structure for the freedom of horseback rides on Cougar Mountain. We'd return after dark, sneaking into the closed kitchen for unsanctioned leftovers. Those happy moments of distance convinced me not to join the house, which would've cemented my commitment in more lasting ways.

During a weekend visit home to Squak Mountain, my mom looked at me from across the kitchen table. "It wasn't the right thing for you," she said about my living situation.

"Why didn't you say so?" My eyes must've looked wide as the uninterrupted skyline I was searching for.

Mom shrugged and didn't look up from her newspapers layered on the table in front of her. "You needed to find out for yourself."

That winter, I moved back to Issaquah and became a commuter student like my brother, leaving a car in the park-and-ride lot and taking the bus to the university district north of downtown. My freshman classes were too large to know anyone well; an hour or two a day spent in this ivy-covered, yet remote, bricked square was not enough to connect in lasting ways. I couldn't wait for what came next.

Several registration forms and advisors later, I enrolled in a new school four and a half hours across the state, the terrain a sharp contrast to the fir and clouds I'd grown up with. Mom and Dad hid any misgivings they might have harbored about a move that hinged on open spaces and horses along with education and helped me pack a car full of clothes and books for my new school, the trees staying behind the further east we drove.

We took the same route Nicole and I'd traveled, this time in a station wagon instead of a convertible and wearing sweatshirts rather than fashionable scarves. The sun still found its way through the car windows for our long drive across Snoqualmie Pass and the Columbia River, the roads narrowing and the towns growing smaller. We sped through the last miles of wheat rustling in the wind that characterized this place, a landscape of migrating students and soil.

The second stage of sustainable farming, alternatives, finds solutions to issues such as soil erosion. Federal initiatives pay farmers not to plow specific plots of land, keeping the soil out of circulation a decade or more. Other alternatives seek entirely new land uses. In a 2007 grant between WSU and the Washington Sustainable Food and Farming Network, farmers raised beef cattle as an alternative to wheat, a moneymaking compromise to farmers who'd set aside land for rejuvenation and native grasses. Through alternatives to conventional practices, farmers blended current agricultural practices with a vision of healthier ecosystems, just as students in the remote college town of Pullman wrestled between their current identities and those they'd grow into.

I'd been assigned a WSU dorm in Stephenson North, the same complex as Nicole's. Hopeful for the friends I'd yet to meet, I hefted boxes of clothes and books into an overused elevator toward the thirteenth floor. My parents and I had just finished lugging up the last boxes when an apologetic resident advisor announced there'd been a mistake, and I was actually assigned to the third floor. Dad's face stayed grim amidst the crowded halls, too many people establishing roots at once in this otherwise quiet corner of the state, solid ground replaced by soil in flux.

Mom took the chaos of the wrong floor in stride. *It'll be okay*, her glance said over the books and clothes we moved all over again. Without sharing my need to roam, she understood the allure of sunny places, like our deck in summer or the light-filled living room where she typed letters to her mom, to her sister, and now that I'd be further from home, to me.

Once the semester began, living in the Palouse grew easier. I studied journalism and wrote about the hills and sky in my spare time. On our regular phone calls, my parents seemed happy with my long-distance adventure. In the days between calls, Mom sent the letters I'd predicted, along with music and snacks for my roommate and me.

During parents' weekend of my first semester, Mom and Dad took me to a restaurant in Idaho, eight miles away. Because the state drinking age at the time was 18, I ordered a daiquiri, the first drink that came to mind. The heavy glass arrived at my table, frosted and pink.

Dad shook his head. "You're in college," he said.

I looked up from my chilled glass.

"You need to drink beer. It's cheaper. And available." Dad sipped from his golden-colored beer, a contrast to the strawberry-pink mixture in front of me. Wheat-based and local, beer was a pragmatic choice, another perspective offered from a region in flux.

Redesign

I rode my bike between Palouse hills, their brown soil bare and ready for fall planting. Highway 270 curved below my dorm, sloping eight miles to Idaho. I only traveled a mile or so along this roadway to reach my horse, a red roan I'd bought when I was seventeen. He lived at the same stable I'd visited a few months earlier with Nicole, the more modest facility closer to campus and accessible by bike.

Only a few cars passed me, the road quiet compared to the busy weekends to come with college students bound for Idaho. The wind pushed me down the last hill to the barnyard, which dipped from the roadside. I visited the roan, named Troj, several afternoons a week, with few other riders in sight. I saw Nicole, who kept her horse several miles down the road, infrequently. While she had her own campus friends and direction, my friends lived in the dorm or worked for the student newspaper.

I'd moved to Washington State University to study writing and journalism. In the past, my words came out lush, like rain, yet this arid climate offered a more economic perspective. Teachers encouraged me to pare my descriptive language, working within the spare landscape rather than struggling against it. I'd write for the school newspaper as a reporter and later as the city editor, covering a college-town crossroads full of students ready to take their chances on a different direction.

My horse, hopeful for carrots, wandered into his stall from the outdoor run. I brushed his sides, dusty from rolling, and combed his thick, red and white-peppered tail. Other horses came inside from their runs in case I might have something for them, too, and stayed watchful even when it turned out I was saddling a horse rather than feeding one.

Like the fruit orchards I'd visited with my parents, the barnyard was compact and no-frills quiet, efficiency underlying its simplicity. Though the wind blew, the soil didn't, convinced to stay put for now. The persistent breeze picked up the scent of plowed earth, reminding me of Mom's garden and its mix of squash and strawberries.

A third phase of sustainable farming, redesign, encourages a stronger commitment to ecological practices through openness to change. Of the three phases, redesign is the least tangible, an ideal to grow toward rather than a specific ending point.

Over the years, farming east of the mountains would encompass a broader view of protection. A vineyard I'd visit in the Yakima Valley twenty-five years later would track not only the wines produced but also the water resources used. This winery, among others, would participate in Salmon Safe habitats, ensuring minimal pesticide use and a maximum of trees along waterways for a safe-fish environment, making the white wine I'd sample all the sweeter.

Most of the state's abundant wheat fields, already suited to the region due to their low water usage, would become known as dryland farms, agricultural centers relying on rainfall rather than irrigation. No-till technology, or planting seeds in previous crop stubble without turning the dirt, would also minimize erosion and help stabilize this region of highly productive, restless soil.

I brushed my horse in the shadow of a hillside, the renewal of the region continuing long after the three years I'd spend here. With a saddle on his back, Troj flicked his ears toward the breeze. Though I'd planned to ride in the corral, its circular borders didn't fit the warm gusts and sky stretching beyond what I could see. I led Troj to the mounting block and tightened the girth with an eye toward the fence-free fields, which farmers allowed us to ride in before the winter wheat planting.

After swinging into the saddle, its leather worn to a practical fit against my legs and seat, I guided Troj away from the arena and pointed him uphill. At our change in direction, the horse broke into a two-beat trot, then a canter. Our climb ended in a rounded peak, its smooth top offering a view of the stable and buildings a few hills away. The horse's hooves sank in the dark soil, enough to root us here for now. We galloped into apricot-colored light, hills multiplying like waves.

6

High-Tech Forest

"Hello?" I repeated into the phone at my first full-time job after college. Back on the western side of the state and in the shadow of Mount Rainier, I worked as a reporter and a photographer for a small-town newspaper. I strained to hear the person I spoke with on the other end of the line, a city official I was interviewing for a story. In a cage behind me, an Amazon parrot named Joey squawked. "Hello?" he asked again, his green head twisted to one side as if he, too, were looking for answers in this rural area on the outskirts of growth and change.

At a weekly newspaper housed in a two-story building on the town's main street, I covered zoning changes, church services, and Friday night football games. I reviewed restaurants offering hometown cooking of chicken and gravy and attended a practice burn dressed in a protective suit, crawling on the floor elbow-to-elbow with firefighters in training. At the new gun range, the staff insisted I try out the guns for full effect and a better story. I fired a .22, and afterward a .45 they told me not to drop when it delivered the promised kickback.

I took pictures and developed them using a darkroom in the back, the film wrapped around a steel wheel and no sign of crumpling, the light turned off after the mistake I'd made flipping the switch and destroying a week's work. The only solution to the ruined film was to take my car on the same route, retaking shots of people and places that weren't quite the same a day or two later. I worried the editor, my boss, would find the photos lackluster or out of focus, my mind wandering outside the boundaries of this small town to other corners of the West.

From a desk near mine, the editor laughed aloud, an outburst making Joey laugh, too, their guffaws bouncing around the thin newsroom walls. I smiled at how human Joey sounded, as if he understood the joke. The length and loudness of his laughter made it tough to write. With a word to my boss about checking the police blotters, I took my notebook and headed out the door, not office-savvy enough to realize it might've been better to laugh a little more and write a little less rather than look for excuses to leave.

In a silver Mustang, I drove out of the parking lot and up into the hills, past the communities of Bonney Lake and Buckley. They were small towns, not unlike Issaquah with its own weekly paper, where I'd interned one semester. While interviewing and writing offered a bird's eye view of people and place, the professional pay was low with no guarantee of benefits. But I had a job, and in an uncertain economy, it was a start, weekly papers undergoing a transition of their own just before the world turned digital. Writers fresh out of school were plentiful.

In Orting, I met a reporter named Lori from a rival, regional paper. She sat in the council chamber a few seats away, the audience sparse on this midweek, midafternoon meeting. "What do you cover?" I asked.

She looked up from her notebook, dark hair set off with a scarf circling her neck. "Mostly Puyallup news, sometimes Orting."

"Are you covering Red Hat Days?" The autumn festival, a tradition rooted in the start of hunting season, created a good feature opportunity. Lori nodded and told me she lived in the area but not in the town she wrote about. Though immersed in these communities during the day, I, too, hadn't made the commitment to live in them full time, torn between career goals and family and friends, who lived further north.

During weekend trips to Issaquah, about forty-five minutes away, I'd visit the Gilman Town Hall Museum, Issaquah's original town hall from the 1890s, and its current museum. Mom worked and volunteered there, even co-chairing the museum. Her working life began after high school with a state job giving loans to farmers. When I worried out loud about my own field, that the writing and office politics weren't what I'd expected, Mom smiled. "You'll never go hungry," she said.

"The jail's open," she'd add in a cheerful tone as if this were a good segue. We walked through a kitchen full of gadgets she'd collected. A sign on the table encouraged visitors to touch the tools as a way of connecting with those who'd worked before us. I picked up black-handled eggbeaters identical to the kind we used at Grandma's, and probably were hers.

In the museum backyard stood a 1914 stone building, the old town jail where Mom led tours of visiting kids. The small cell held a bunk, a chamber pot, and not much else. Past the stout thick concrete of the jail, the yard was lined with yellow and pink roses. Mom stopped to inspect the flowerbeds before leading us back inside to the exhibits.

A chart in the front of the museum talked about the Native Americans who first lived in the region, how Issaquah was a Native American place name meaning "the sound of water birds." Sammamish people were among early residents of the valley, camping on the shores of the lake that eventually would be named for them. The first white Americans came in the 1860s. Attracted by the area's valley farmland, they planted hops. Farmers employed both white and Native American workers, some from the eastern side of the mountains. Life in the small community was not always peaceful—in a tragic 1885 event, hops pickers killed three Chinese laborers. Coal mining and the railroad helped the town boom, while I-90 split through town and brought more residents to this bedroom community, over time becoming a place to live and work in its own right.

The town of Orting, with a similar start to Issaquah in hops and logging, now sold flower bulbs and Christmas trees. During a sunny Red Hat Days, Lori and I prowled the festival grounds on foot for news from the parade, the participants, and town officials. One of the Red Hat Days staff recognized us and took us aside. "How would you two like to judge the baby contest?" The woman's eyes were confident, her smile wide as the cloud-free sky on that fall day. She must've realized it'd be impossible to turn her down.

Lori and I let the woman escort us to a shaded pavilion where we judged dimpled babies presented by hopeful moms and dads. Any decision we made would please the winning parents alone, making me squirm like the infants we judged. Lori looked just as concerned, though she handled this unexpected job with grace, taking careful notes, city council-style, in front of each smiling, anxious parent. We conspired and whispered, our rival newspaper status forgotten.

A few council meetings later, Lori and I moved into a townhouse apartment in Federal Way, a town close to our newspaper beats and within reach of Seattle and Tacoma. With both of us new in our careers, we saved money in different ways, like stocking the fridge with boxed wine and turning on the oven rather than using the heat to warm our hands after late night council meetings. One of us put liquid detergent in the dishwasher, making a blizzard of bubbles across the kitchen floor.

While Lori stayed with her newspaper job, mine didn't last. Downsized, I questioned if journalism was the path for me, if I could handle assignments like the photograph of a wrecked car whose seventeen-year-old driver didn't survive, a scene I'd kept my distance from. I worked jobs for a temporary agency and plotted—one foot rooted in where I was from and the journalism I'd studied, the other poised for chance and the lure of what lie past the mountains.

Through the spacious Boeing parking lot in south Seattle, site of my latest temporary assignment, I showed a badge to a man at the booth and found my way to a cubicle. Because my group worked early, I came in first thing, too, sneaking up to the cafeteria to buy a pastry before clocking in. In a building so tall it looked as if it might have once housed an airplane, I edited documents for a boss who valued clean, crisp language. This paring of words wasn't a stretch from the journalism I'd studied, just a more controlled narrative with a different audience. Engineers came by my cube to sharpen their content, keeping it within the margins even as I wondered about my own boundaries, how far they might stretch.

Originally from Detroit, Michigan, William Boeing moved to the Northwest, starting a lumber company in Hoquiam (HO kwe um), Washington, in 1903. From his initial success, he cultivated an interest in aviation over the next few years, and along with Conrad Westervelt, a Navy lieutenant, and Herb Munter, a young pilot, built an airplane called *Bluebill*. Boeing officially started his company in 1916, selling *Bluebill* and a second plane, *Mallard*, to a New Zealand company in 1919. Following WWI, the young company encountered difficult times, causing it to diversify into other products, such as furniture. In the decades following, the company grew to one of the largest employers in the Northwest, building planes for the military in World War II, planes to carry the mail, and eventually, commercial aircraft.

When Dad graduated from a college in Massachusetts with an electrical engineering degree, there were no jobs in sight. He returned to the papermill where he'd grown up, some work better than none, and sent out a round of applications. Boeing offered him a position. In 1951, Dad drove with a friend across the country on Route 66, toward a job he thought would be a milestone on his eventual journey back east. His friend ended up staying in the Northwest for a year before returning home. Dad stayed for one year and then the next, building a thirty-seven-year career of work on planes such as the B50, the C97 cargo plane, the 707, Air Force One for President Kennedy, the 747, and the 767.

In the early 1970s, Boeing faced an economic crisis. With the SST program cancelled and no new orders coming in, the company laid off more than half its workforce, a shift from 80,000 employees to 37,200. Because of limited opportunities, many left the area, prompting the famous billboard, "Will the last person leaving SEATTLE—Turn out the lights." Some, Dad among them, survived the layoffs, adapting to leaner times.

The version of Boeing I walked into had adapted, too, with numerous planes and plants in more than one place, along with workers who lived both in urban areas and the suburbs. One of my coworkers lived on a houseboat, a home she showed me at lunchtime one day. Her commute from office to boat was brief, water never too far no matter what part of Seattle one worked in. Comfortable with the boat's gentle motion, she set plates on a compact table and handed me a napkin. I imagined this coworker's ability to live in more than one place, a threshold wherever she docked her boat, considering the same kind of life for myself.

Down a glassy hallway of a new temporary position, I passed an office with a guitar hanging from the ceiling. Another coworker arranged toys in a wading pool near his desk. Microsoft, unlike some of the other contract positions I'd been assigned to, favored the eccentric over the structured; office playgrounds proved more frequent than straightforward cubicles.

During this high-tech boom, Microsoft chose a forested area in Redmond for its headquarters, a city on the other side of Lake Washington from Seattle. Campus-like, the office buildings had benches scattered outside. Employees, some of them wearing shorts even if the weather was in the 60s, took breaks or held meetings in these small courtyards.

I worked from an inner part of the X-shaped building, across the hall from windowed, decorated offices belonging to programmers and senior employees. Because temporary workers claimed the office I worked in, the walls stayed bare, nobody remaining in the room long enough to personalize it and make it their own. My mentor and officemate, also a contract worker, didn't seem to notice the spare quality of our environment, our assigned task filling the space for her.

Greeting me from a tangle of hair, my mentor set me up with a style sheet to format instructional documents. "You'll find the style codes here," she said, pointing to an online listing. Though bright light shone through windows on the far side of the X, our room stayed dim despite the fluorescent overheads and a desk lamp.

I spent full days formatting documents and socializing with my co-workers, who worked eight hours and longer. Most of the time, I worked alongside them to meet deadlines and product releases. I applied new styles, unchecked by my mentor, whose focus stayed locked on her screen. I wondered if people would read the words I massaged or if they'd react like me, diving into a program and clicking icons until something happened.

A row of offices stayed lit one evening, computer glow multiplying down my arm of the X. I highlighted a paragraph, popping the required margins and styles in place. Guitar sounds mixed with voices from one of the offices. Text on the screen blurred, my eyes tiring. I blinked, forcing the words to stay still, but the paragraphs in front of me wavered like the wading pool a few doors down.

"I think I'll call it a night," I told my mentor.

"Okay," she said without looking up, her glasses fixed on a printed manual beside her monitor.

I walked downstairs, the glassed reception area darkened from sunset. The front desk stood empty, the receptionist having already left a few hours ago. At the building entrance, I noticed someone outside opening the glass door at the same time I was leaving. Rather than meandering through the parking lot strewn with trees to find a place for his car, the sandy-haired man had parked right up front, as if he owned the place. I fiddled with my bag and looked up again, my steps slowing to focus on this man who looked like Bill Gates.

He fumbled with the door, giving me time to plan the things I'd say about the contract work, his company, all the trees he'd left. His face stayed shy, pleading with me to say nothing. He held the door open, my day ending while his was just beginning. I imagined his shy smile was as much for the place as it was for me in this organization he'd built, a workplace he loved. I slipped into the parking lot full of trees with a single word, *thanks*.

Trees filled the window of my new office in Austin all the way to the river where a bridge arched across it, a scene easy to get lost in. Although I didn't have a guitar to hang up or a wading pool to inflate, unwilling to go too far too soon, I'd tacked up some posters and placed a few office trinkets on my desk. It was enough to personalize the space, which I shared with no one. After a series of temporary jobs and a close call but no concrete, full-time offer, I left my home in Washington for a forest filled with new types of trees, juniper and live oak. My job here was editing, similar to positions at Microsoft and Boeing. Like the other places I'd worked, the engineers were reluctant to bring me their work at first, warming up to the process once I explained the changes I'd make, how I'd pare the words to what was essential.

Across the country, the high-tech forest exploded in the early 1990s, with Internet and e-mail use becoming as commonplace as office politics and fresh coffee. In this latest corporate culture to be deciphered, it was okay to socialize with coworkers, acceptable to know them in the interests of working well together. While I'd moved to Austin, Lori had moved to California, both of us writing yet in different ways than we'd imagined. Everyone was suddenly from somewhere else, a work migration born of economic necessity and adventure.

On one of my trips home, I stopped in the Gilman Town Hall Museum on a quiet Saturday. I browsed through the books for names I remembered, friends of Mom's such as Harriet Fish, who helped establish the Issaquah Historical Society in the early 1970s. A columnist, Fish wrote about preserving the area's historical sites and artifacts in the *Issaquah Press* and illustrated a book of local history, *Past at Present*, written by her husband, Edwards. She was also the first woman member of the Issaquah school board. Fish later moved to the town of Sequim, located on the Olympic Peninsula. In a letter, Mom told me about a visit to Harriet. I imagined the stories they must've talked about, the past's covert hold on the present.

In the gift section, I found small stacks of note cards Harriet Fish had drawn. One showed a sketch of Pickering Barn, a stable in Issaquah where I'd ridden horses named Scout and Touché. The barn, which now hosted a farmer's market, rested in a shopping center rather than the neighboring skyport that skydivers used to jump into, their parachutes popping onto the field like flowers. For a news story, I'd ridden in a glider and floated above Issaquah, the flight soundless over pasture land and cows in the valley floor.

"I grew up here." I smiled at the museum docent and showed her the note cards I wanted to buy.

The woman waited, her nod matching the tentative gray skies outside. "No one is from here," she said with a straight face, adding that she and her husband had moved here a few years ago.

I listened to the assurance of her words, the note cards between us capturing the town in a pen-and-ink past. Given American culture's restless geographic changes, the docent had probably met few people who'd hadn't moved here for the lure of a new position or a renewed perspective, home a harder place to find.

1

UPSTREAM

I wove between waves of festival-goers in my hometown, all making their way up Front Street like Chinook salmon returning from the ocean to Issaquah Creek. I was late for my shift selling popcorn at the city's Salmon Days festival, an event I'd attended since grade school. Driving around Seattle with my boyfriend Barry, my hometown commitment was lost in plans of where I'd go next, the new places I'd discover beyond the familiar mountains and rain.

The Issaquah Historical Society's old-fashioned popcorn cart, its windows full of puffed kernels, stood out from neighboring booths selling glass earrings or hand-carved boxes in smooth-grained red and gold. Artists showed paintings of the Puget Sound in thick-textured waves, their blue tint ready to leap off the canvas and splash us.

"There you are," Mom said. Her face held more relief than reproach.

"Sorry." My face warmed. She'd forgiven my lateness too soon, unaware I was plotting a larger escape.

In grade school, I'd placed salmon made of sword ferns into our backyard stream on a route I longed to follow. The stream spilled down Squak Mountain, falling into town where Issaquah Creek flowed. In deeper waters, young salmon swam beside those born in the town hatchery built in 1936 as a public works project to replenish salmon diminished by industry, now one of the most frequently visited hatcheries in the state. The hatchery raised eggs to year-old fish, or smolt. Once released, the young salmon began a journey from Issaquah Creek toward Lake Sammamish, the Sammamish River, Lakes Washington and Union, the Lake Washington Ship Canal, Puget Sound, and the Strait of Juan de Fuca, all to reach the Pacific Ocean.

Without mentioning the trips Barry and I'd planned, I helped Mom scoop bags full of popcorn to waiting customers. Issaquah was poised for restless change, its 1980 population of 5,000 turned close to 8,000 a scant ten years later. The Northwest salmon, meanwhile, were in decline since their peak in the early twentieth century, a loss attributed by scientists to loss of habitat, overfishing, and climate change.

The sun streamed overhead, a warmer October than usual. Visitors were as apt to wear shorts as long pants, trading raingear for light sweatshirts and sunglasses. We watched our popcorn-eating customers head toward Issaquah Creek's returning salmon, fish battling their way home even as I planned slipping away from it.

"Where are the meadows?" I'd asked Dad years ago. Thin alders on Squak Mountain made an opening in the sky, the closest thing to a clearing I'd found in this mix of Douglas fir, ferns, and logs softening back to dirt. Though I dreamed of the clearings described in the books I read, what lured me most was a mental landscape, a place where thoughts, like the horses I rode, broke free and kicked up dust.

"The terrain here isn't built that way," Dad said in a reasoned tone of the soft moss and evergreens around us. I didn't understand I was searching for a region closer to the Southwest or even the East Coast, the home he'd left in his twenties for a job at Boeing in the Pacific Northwest.

After we'd finished our shift, Mom and I joined the rest of the crowd streaming to the hatchery. Past the onlookers on the bridge, we stopped at the holding tanks to see young fish due for release in a year or two. Hatchery smolt would join wild salmon on a complex route of lakes and narrow straits to the cold gray of the ocean, salmon programmed to leave.

The Guadalupe, my first river in Central Texas, was cold as the day was hot, a contrast I wasn't prepared for in this new territory of an adopted home. Cicadas buzzed in the woods alongside the water, a backdrop to shouts from my new coworkers waiting in doughnut-like inner tubes.

"Just jump in," one of them urged. He splashed water on the tube to cool it down before resting his arms on its smooth sides.

My feet, bundled in water sandals, adjusted to the water's cold bite before I sat down fast in my waiting tube, its black sides warmed in the sun. A hidden current pulled me to the rest of the group on this river float, all of us meandering between banks of cypress and lounging green turtles.

One of the shelled creatures swam several feet away, neck up and home just below the surface. It took turtles years to reach maturity, making it challenging for them to reach adulthood—predators' appetites for eggs presented another hurdle. Along with natural causes, changes in the landscape impacted turtles as well. Some varieties, such as the Cagle's map turtle, were candidates for an endangered species listing due to fluctuations in temperature, habitat, and food supply.

The week I arrived in Texas with Barry, the landscape felt just as altered. Sick from July heat, too much barbeque, and the shock of a new place turned home, I'd holed up in a dark hotel room. While Barry learned the ropes at his new job, I stayed wrapped in sheets with curtains drawn tight to block out a determined sun and no sign of rain. On the afternoon news, television anchor Judy Maggio shared reports of a youthful city with paths of water I'd yet to find.

The spring-fed Guadalupe River began in the Hill Country of Central Texas, winding southwest toward the Gulf Coast. Barry and I had journeyed in the same direction from Seattle to reach the Austin hotel Barry's new employer had arranged. In my mid-twenties and without any good job prospects at home, I tagged along to learn the rhythms of an unfamiliar place, turning strangers into friends and adding new versions of weather and wildlife to those I'd grown up with. Leaving my apartment on the south shores of Lake Washington, I didn't want to see the resignation in my parents' eyes, Mom saying less than usual and Dad making room in the Mustang for my house plants while ignoring Barry, who'd suggested I leave them behind.

During my first adventure away from home at Washington State University, I steered a paddleboat across Idaho's Lake Coeur d'Alene with three other students. In 1982, the same year I transferred colleges, Chinook salmon were introduced to Lake Coeur d'Alene. The Idaho Department of Fish and Game stocked the salmon in hopes of having them compete and even prey on the lake's overpopulated kokanee, along with adding to the lake's sports fishing. The new fish thrived in this place that wasn't their home better than anyone had hoped, even creating their own new journeys to area streams to spawn. The lake fish, thriving like their ocean-bound young cousins further west, made the most of the new terrain.

Halfway across the lake, I calculated how long it might take us to reach the other side. The lake was several miles wide and twenty-five meandering miles long. Though our student newspaper retreat at Camp Larson was supposed to help us dream up a semester's worth of stories, we spent just as much time plotting trouble. I'm not sure whose idea it was to take the paddleboat across the lake at dusk, but once we started, there was no stopping, not even for a sun dipping lower against the hillsides. On the opposite shore, beer signs from a dockside bar twinkled closer with each stroke.

"We'll have a beer on the other side," one of us laughed.

After forty-five minutes of paddling, we were close enough to see the bar's patrons, deep into happy hour and watching our progress from an outdoor deck. One of them snorted. A woman, her laugh ragged with cigarettes, took over where the snort left off. A few others shook their heads at our foolishness. The disbelief in their faces reminded us we'd need to make the same ill-advised trip back—this time, in the dark. With the lake's gray waves turned black satin, stopping for a drink didn't seem such a good idea anymore. Though we had life jackets, we had no light, meaning we couldn't see out and other boaters couldn't see us.

With some strategic paddling, we angled the boat for our return trip. Before we could leave, a mustached man in his thirties idled a small motorboat beside us. "I'll tow you back." His tone was loud and a little too confident, as if the beer he'd already drank spoke for him.

"What do you think?" I whispered to my friends. Rather than taking an hour to cross the lake in the dark, this guy, whether he'd been drinking or not, could get us there a lot quicker.

One of us took the length of rope offered by the mustached man and tied it to an unseen loop at the front of the paddleboat. A light from the now-silent motorboat glowed like the moon we didn't have that night.

The mustached man stepped to the front of his craft and revved the engine. "Ready?" His motorboat muttered faster against the waves and growled to life, taking up the slack on our already tensing paddleboat. The four of us onboard waited, unsure. For the first time that day, the adventure was out of our hands. I didn't know what to think in the dark, the lights from the bar bobbing and diving. Freshly placed Chinook in Lake Coeur d'Alene must've felt just as disoriented, with a route to home they could no longer find.

The front of the paddleboat, instead of following the motorboat across the water, took a nosedive under. All four of us moved to the back of the boat and yelled *stop* until the mustached man heard and cut his engine. One of our guys slipped the connecting rope off the front of the paddleboat and into the water before it could dip any further under.

The mustached man idled his motorboat close by. "We'll tie it in another place." He started to refigure the rope.

The paddleboat answered with a quiet drifting of its own, away from the motorboat and the man crouched inside it.

"That's all right," a voice on our boat said, letting the man know we'd had enough and would try it on our own.

The mustached man frowned. "It's pretty dark out there." He waited, a wavering shape against the bar's neon lights, for us to change our minds. "Lots of drunks on the lake."

Like you, I wanted to say.

"Thanks for your help, but we'll be all right," someone else in our group said. "We made it this far, we'll make it back."

I hoped he was right. Though our camp probably had a phone number, none of us knew it. Docking the boat and traveling by land would take miles, maybe all night, not to mention we didn't know our way in this new place. The bar onlookers who'd watched us earlier had moved inside with their beer and jokes, fresh stories to share about college kids in a paddleboat.

Heading for the opposite shore, the four of us sang as loud as we could to steady our nerves and keep stray boaters from running into us. With every turn I took paddling, my legs locked in repetition and intent. We made it about a third of the way across when another boat sputtered close. My feet froze on the paddles. All singing stopped, one of us calling out "hello, hello!"

This driver, unlike the mustached man, stopped a safe distance away from the paddleboat. "I'll stay beside you," a man's voice offered.

No one said a thing, not even to each other. "That'd be great," someone said at last, the words quiet in all that darkness.

This driver shadowed our paddleboat like an angel, his craft spilling dusty light across the water for us to follow. Beneath the waves our boats made, underwater shadows hovered through the night, Chinook salmon testing their own boundaries.

At Barton Springs, created millions of years ago in shifting terrain, I toed the water without committing. Though its deep green surface could be mistaken for warm, the springs, a consistent sixty-eight to seventy-one degrees year round, provided a chilly respite to the summer heat. Contained by a small, manmade dam in 1929, Barton Springs Pool sustained both human swimmers and a variety of aquatic life, including an endangered salamander and several types of turtles. Despite the Austin-San Marcos area's unabashed population growth, with a 47 percent increase from 1990–2000 and a 37 percent increase from 2000–2010, wildlife in the springs survived through a combination of protection and resilience.

In the years since I'd moved to Central Texas, I'd expanded my education, career, and social life, punctuated with tubing trips along the Guadalupe and San Marcos Rivers or swimming in Lake Travis. A few times, I went sailing, learning knots and doing my best to anticipate the fickle boom, which lurched across the deck whenever the mood struck. My personal relationships were just as hard to predict.

After Barry and I stopped seeing each other, I dated a friend-of-a-friend for several years, so busy with work and a slow-going master's degree that I didn't see the relationship as I might have, its foundation murky. In our early thirties, we married, a union lasting just over a year. I spent the next few years dating or on my own, rivers and area pools a cold solace and clear escape. With the security my job editing marketing materials offered and the satisfaction of school and horseback riding, I stayed rooted in this place, poised for a growth spurt of its own.

The crowd at Barton Springs Pool applauded a twisting dive, the board still reverberating from the youth's jump. Beside me, a father urged a youngster into the cold. Teenagers slapped water at one another. Native Americans called Barton Springs the "Sacred Springs," a healing place. On one visit to a trail running parallel to the springs, I'd spotted a mottled snake coiled along the shore on a bed of rocks placed to help prevent erosion. Red-tailed hawks hunted the shores and Great Egrets posed in the water. The banks of the springs were lined with grasses and elm, a good habitat for birds and the open spaces I'd always looked for, the meadows I'd searched for in the forest.

Slipping down the rock moss, I sank into the springs and the icy shock of the water, a breathless moment fading with the quick movements of swimming. Once my breathing slowed to normal, I swam to the middle of the springs, just far enough from the diving board and couples splashing water at one another. A green turtle joined me, gliding with purpose across the width of the pool. I kept my distance so I wouldn't interrupt her journey. Although female turtles can travel great lengths on land to find an appropriate nest, they also have an established home range, bound-aries they're comfortable with. I edged closer, enough to make her uneasy and dive deeper into safer algae and rocks. I swam beside her the last sec-ond or two, past the voices around us, into waters nearly as cold as those I'd grown up with.

Outside my childhood home on Squak Mountain, the backyard stream rumbled thick and loud from fall rain. I inhaled the damp ground and slipped into Dad's car beside John, a musician I'd met through a setup and my husband for the past two years. John, who shared my interest in com-ing to the Northwest, could see past the clouds.

I'd offered to make jambalaya, meaning a trip to town for ingredients. "We'll stop by the festival," I said to John during our drive. Traveling in fall rather than summer gave us a chance to see the vine maple change from green to gold and to feel the air tinged with cold. It was the first weekend in October, and the salmon were returning.

After the fifteen-minute drive to town, we left the car at the park-and-ride lot and took a bus to the annual Salmon Days festival, which, like my hometown, was still growing. Issaquah's population, now around 15,000, had tripled from the time I'd grown up there, changing as much as I had.

Both our faces tightened, John from the crowds, mine from the extra time this errand might take. "It'll be worth it," I promised myself as much as John. I led us up through the center of the festival on Front Street, the place Mom and I had sold popcorn. Though our stand was long gone, I stopped at one of the booths to admire its jewelry.

John stood a few paces away, keeping a distance. "We should get back."

I took his hand and moved away from booths of earrings and artwork, heading for Sunset Way and the fish hatchery. Years ago, I'd traded the present for dreams of new places—coming back, I was reluctant to leave.

At the same time, we needed to run our errands. "We have time to see the salmon." Two coho salmon statues rested larger-than-life on rock ped-estals, celebrating the continuation of the salmon runs and the longevity of the hatchery despite a near-closure in the early 1990s due to budget cuts. In 1994, the nonprofit Friends of the Issaquah Salmon formed as an advocate of the hatchery and a provider of educational opportunities for visitors. State protections in 1999 ensured further preservation and resto-ration of the salmon habitat.

We waited our turn at the crowded bridge across the creek, its shores framed by reddened vine maple and a few alders. The air above the water smelled of moss and rain. Biologists claim the salmon find their way home by the unique scent of their spawning grounds. In the ocean, it's less clear which senses the fish rely on to find their particular stream. From an opening on the railing, we gained a close-up view of the salmon, scales glinting and mouths gaping from their fight against the current. Many of the adult salmon jumped up the fish ladder and into the Issaquah Creek basin to spawn, while others would be harvested by the hatchery for their eggs. After spawning, both wild and hatchery adults would die.

In addition to keeping a careful balance between wild and hatchery salmon, river health and accessibility were also vital issues for the fish and a work in progress as the area shifted and grew. Plans included replacement of an aging dam on Issaquah Creek along with adding weirs, which are easier for salmon to find their way back.

We walked across the bridge and past the fish ladder of leaping salmon, bodies arcing in the afternoon sun. At a hatchery holding tank, adult coho and Chinook drifted past one another, ready to spawn another generation of restless journeys. Despite this altered habitat, the salmon were maintaining their numbers in more than one location, creating more than one kind of home.

On our way back, I lingered at the bridge, which now had plenty of openings at the rail. We watched the salmon, scales like shields, battle upstream to the home they'd left, certain in their return.

8
Last Light on North Beach

Our car sped toward the beach, hurtling down the freeway in a race against sunset. "I'd like to see the ocean again," I'd said an hour earlier, setting the family sedan in motion once I realized my aunt and uncle, whom we were visiting on the Olympic Peninsula, lived only about an hour away from it. All five of us—Mom, Dad, Aunt Delores, Uncle Red, and I—talked about the idea a little too long, losing precious light before we piled into the car and headed onto Highway 101 toward Copalis Beach. Although I'd visited the sunny Gulf Coast of my new life in Central Texas, I missed the brooding, dark-sanded beaches of childhood vacations, the actual place and the past mixed together until it wasn't clear which I was looking for.

Copalis Beach, north of the Columbia River on the Olympic Peninsula, had been shifting all along in quiet increments, its shores and rivers altered by human influence. In recent years, a strong El Niño pattern of winds and rain battered the Washington shoreline, moving sandy boundaries even further past memory.

Dad drove the sedan with Red up front, both of them staring at maps and forecasting the least congested route on freeways and side roads. In the back seat, I stayed comfortable beside Mom, Delores on the other side. They had their own summer stories of the north beaches, my aunt remembering falling asleep to the sound the waves made. Another time, their dad coaxed the sisters outside in the middle of the night to watch the fireworks show he'd set up for them in the sand, roman candles and rockets mixing with the stars.

Their vacations on water stretched inland to Olympia with lakeside picnics, black-and-white photos showing Mom standing on a dock with people labeled in captions as friends. Behind the easy smiles and calm water, Mom had nearly drowned as a child, the reason behind our frequent swimming lessons.

From the car, I watched the horizon, clear except for strips of cloud, sunset about forty-five minutes away. This break from work and school gave me a chance to visit past landscapes to see if the view was any different. We zoomed past evergreens, their trunks and moss-green branches blurring to gray.

"Do you think we'll make it?" I asked Mom.

"We're getting close," she said, just as she might've years ago, as if I'd asked *how much further?*

On the straightaway, Dad drove even faster. Few cars passed us on this midweek drive, most travelers having already arrived. I tried not to see the lower slant of light. Sunset came later this far north, I reasoned, wrapping my fingers around the seatbelt. Soon, if the scenery matched memory, trees and underbrush would give way to tide flats, more clouds, and waves tumbling over one another, playful as children.

My past was wrapped up in the small condo we'd stay at each summer. Part of a 1960s complex with sliding glass doors, sandy carpet, and a fold-out bed for me, some units were near the pool, while others had a view of the ocean. After setting down our bags, we'd drive to a Copalis store offering whole chickens crisp under an orange lamp and homemade bread, still warm, in brown loaves. Pushing a creaking cart on the wood floor, Mom picked up practical items like milk and spaghetti, staples that always tasted better at the beach than they did at home.

Once the groceries were unpacked, we'd change into swimsuits and run for the beach, taunting chilled waves with bare feet and forgetting how cold it was, even on summer days. Ken and I edged past the foam when our legs numbed enough not to feel the water, our hair slicked back from the constant wind. I'd end up with water to my waist, enough to float the gentler waves back to shore. To warm up, Mom and I read under one of the dunes, the wind's constant sigh a background to wherever our books happened to take us that day.

After a day or so exploring the more remote Copalis Beach, we'd drive to nearby Ocean Shores for shopping and a walk on the jetty. Wearing a hooded sweatshirt, a necessity then and a fashion statement in years to come, I jumped rocks on the North Jetty, a finger of black boulders jutting into the ocean. While Mom read in a drift of sand, Ken and I, both in grade school, searched the tiny pools the waves made, now filled with crustaceans and plant life. Other sea life lingered close—from a point near the jetty, Dad once spotted a whale, its gray form moving like a wave.

"Let's walk to the end," I'd say to Ken, pointing to the rocks at the furthest tip of a narrowing spit.

Like the shifting currents beneath its surface, the jetty's reach traveled farther than I thought. The Ocean Shores community of hotels, restaurants, and souvenir shops rested on a sandy strip formed largely by the jetty we stood on. Constructed in the early 1900s to improve ship navigation in Grays Harbor, the jetty helped redirect the sand, spurring area growth and tourism. In more recent years, the sand-building pattern had stalled, even reversing itself through erosion. Findings of a Southwest Washington Coastal Erosion Study suggested the jetties, which caused the initial growth of sand, were now also responsible for its reversal.

Climate change and shifting weather also played a role in the coastal erosion, influencing the shores since the early 1900s. The aptly named Washaway Beach, located south of Ocean Shores in Westport, averages about 100 feet of erosion per year and is called the fastest eroding beach on the Pacific Coast. After coastal storms, news reports would show another abandoned cabin falling into the sea, summer memories washed from sight.

With scenery flying by, Dad made good time to the town of Aberdeen on Grays Harbor, a landmark on our route and birthplace of musician Kurt Cobain. Although most summer trips to the beach had included a stop in this harbor town for a burger or a slice of blackberry pie, we were racing the sun with no time for lingering.

The city streets looked the same as I'd remembered the past twenty-some years, with small retail shops and a lone logging truck rumbling by, a tiny red flag attached to the longest felled tree. The area's ample natural resources had drawn people here for years. The Lower Chehalis Tribe lived on saltwater fish and used the region's abundant timber for canoes. White Americans arriving in the mid-1800s established a logging industry in a town that bustled until the 1980s. Facing dwindling resources and mill closures, the town has since shifted its focus toward retail and tourism.

Dad drove straight ahead, his view unwavering. There wouldn't be time to consider a bridge near the Wishkah River, where Cobain was said to have spent time, or to drive by some of the schools he'd attended.

I harbored my own Aberdeen memory of a family trip to the beach where my best grade school friend was supposed to meet us. After her parents dropped her off in Aberdeen, my parents would take her the rest of the way to the beach, an ocean sleepover.

At our prearranged café, I remember looking out the window for a sign of my friend bouncing from her dad's white pickup. Too many other cars came and left, the roads punctuated by logging trucks. Mom and Dad had already finished their lunch. I lingered, buying time and hopeful my parents hadn't noticed how late she was. Mom stirred her hot tea in slow circles, as if she, too, were stalling.

After the server cleared the last plates, Dad stared into the parking lot along with me. An hour past our meeting point, he turned back to the table. "I'll drive back to Issaquah and pick her up."

Mom shook her head, "It's too far." She was right, of course, about what amounted to a seven-hour round trip. I didn't see it then, nor did I see the longer distance my friend would need to navigate with her parents, whose fierce arguments drove us under the covers during sleepovers at her house. Mom and Dad stood up, prepared to leave without her. Dad's mouth set in a line, my own expression dark as the Pacific. For years after that, Aberdeen held that association for me, the same overcast skies I heard in Cobain's music.

Dad accelerated the sedan, prepared to speed through Aberdeen and hook north before the sun slipped into the ocean, not waiting for anyone this time, no time for disappointment. Storefronts whizzed past, with a single logging roaring inland. Finding traffic, our sedan slowed to a more sedate crawl.

I looked around for the police and found none, just a line of cars and a bridge. At the front of the line, a bridge lifted toward the sky. A drawbridge, a necessity in this confluence of two rivers and a harbor, stood wide open to let a vessel sail through. In all our years of vacations, I never once saw the bridge open at the exact moment we were about to across; in fact I barely remember it. Even now, Dad captures the moment better than me.

"It was all we needed," he'd say, shaking his head as if still seeing the bridge open midair, a ship passing in slow motion front of us.

With the bridge back in place and traffic on the move, proximity to the beach boosted our morale, the shoreline in sight with ships like toys on the horizon. Though Dad and Ken sometimes took fishing trips during our family vacations, a beached ship near Ocean Shores, the *S.S. Catala*, was the vessel I spent the most time on. A photo shows me as a teenager in a gray sweatshirt and jeans, leaning on its sloping deck. Other visitors balanced on the ship's sand-bleached boards and peered into parts of the vessel covered in graffiti.

Built in 1925, the *S.S. Catala* initially transported passengers in British Columbia, and was dubbed the "Logger's Liner" by the Washington Department of Ecology. Taken out of service in the late 1950s, it became a floating hotel for Seattle's World's Fair. In 1963, it began a new life at Ocean Shores, where it again served as a hotel and restaurant for visiting beach-goers. On New Year's Day, 1965, a storm with winds of seventy miles an hour and nine-foot swells flooded and later beached the ship. Deemed too expensive to rescue, the ship was left in the sand for years, drawing visitors like us to its tilting slope, a slanted homecoming.

I walked in careful steps across the deck with other explorers prowling alongside me. Dad, who climbed around the ship with Ken and me, showed me how to align the viewfinder not with him, but with the angle of the deck. Pictures showed the optical illusion he'd been after, his body leaning at forty-five degrees. Graffiti peppered the metal wall behind him and two holes the size of a large shoebox punctuated the deck, a place we wouldn't be allowed to prowl today.

A few years after we took the pictures, parts of the ship began disappearing. The signature red and white stacks, removed in 1980, were the first to go. Soon after, officials buried the remaining abandoned hull in the sand. Another visitor to the ship, which was reexposed through shifting sands, poked a hole in its side in 2006 and discovered 34,000 gallons of fuel tank oil that had been there all along. Over a period of nearly a year and a half, the state Department of Ecology worked with four other agencies to remove the fuel tank oil along with treating 360,000 gallons of oily water. Workers took what remained of the *S.S. Catala* away, restoring the coastline and averting disaster for area birds and wildlife.

Just before sunset, the sedan rounded the last turn of the tide flats, beach trips from the past crowding close. We smelled the ocean before we saw it, the seagulls turning orange and pink in the softening light. Rather than taking time to find the old resort, Dad parked on a public spot. We were the sole car in the small, sandy space in front of wooden piers and a sign stating "walking only."

With the gentle slamming of doors, we stepped outside the car into sunset and no time to waste. I passed out sweatshirts to Mom and Delores for the insistent wind and dropping temperatures. A set of waves crashed in our direction and left just as fast, sighing over leftover driftwood and sand.

"We barely made it," Dad said.

"But we're here," Mom said.

Daylight offered a scant twenty minutes or so for an ocean walk. A few other people wandered closer to the water, their shapes silhouetted. A dog barked behind its owners, as if to hurry them along.

On one of our last family trips to the beach, Dad I had walked toward a distant rock with mist at its base and clouds in the distance, a goal I set for us. "It's farther than it looks," Dad warned, but headed that direction with me anyway, the ocean roaring to our left and daylight on our right. Mom, who'd been with us for the first part of the walk, chose the path to the condo instead. The tide was out, the water revealing a wide berth of wet sand, the kind easiest to walk on. Though our steps seemed closer to our goal, the lights on this faraway shore didn't change much, the mist-shrouded distance we needed to cover deceptive.

At dusk, we reached a sandbar and the closest we'd come to the pointed rock, now bordered by a dark width of water that was probably the Copalis River. The towering milestone with its lone tree looked more distinct, yet still out of reach. A muted sunset made us realize we'd have to walk home in the dark. Guided by the ocean's rumbling and lights further inland, we hiked back the way we'd come, the Beachwood Resort's squat lookout tower guiding us between the dunes.

This uninterrupted route along the shore wouldn't last. Twenty years later, the nearby Connor Creek began changing course. Redirected by the Army Corps of Engineers after veering too close to shoreline development, the Connor had the last word by creating its own, more drastic course across the sand. Its north-south course soon severed shore access in this area altogether. A footbridge built across the creek became the only means of reaching the ocean, a final link to a more distant past.

On packed sand, Dad, Red, and I walked along green waves, retreating with the tide. Mom and Delores followed in easy steps, content to slow down now that we'd arrived. I took off my shoes, my toes ready for the cold froth. Behind us, wet outlines of my footprints filled faster than I made them. In the years to come, I'd bring John to this ocean beach, eager to show him the dark sand and ignoring the cars that now drove along the shoreline. We'd search for a childhood restaurant farther up the coast, which by then would be long gone, although John found a wood auction in Copalis and bought two carved bears, making fresh connections here rather than getting caught up in distant ones.

Walking on the shore with my parents, aunt, and uncle in those last bits of light, it was easy to fall into old ways and search for perfect shells, unblemished remembrances. Yellow kelp curled into whips on the wet shore, ridged dunes shapeless as memory. Though the water and sand felt the same, the towns and shorelines near them were changing, shifting all along. The last moments of daylight tipped the breakers in fire before turning deeper gray to match the sand, the new waves we'd found already fading from sight.

9

VISITS FROM BLACK BEAR

On the outskirts of a park near downtown Seattle, a mountain lion slipped between the trees. His visit to this urban area coincided with my own late summer visit to Squak Mountain, about twenty miles east. No one was sure how a young male mountain lion, his amber coat interrupted with a shadowed face, found his way into an urban park and a neighborhood called Magnolia. A mountain lion roaming the middle of the city wasn't anything I'd ever heard of growing up here, despite our occasional wildlife neighbors such as deer and bear. Over the years, most of our feline encounters came from housecats like Muppet, Binky, and Fritz, which adopted us one by one.

Black Bear, a cat Mom found lanky and stray at a nearby diner, was the pet most torn between indoors and out. After my parents visited this restaurant with its home cooking and paintings of mountain scenery, the cat would be at the entryway, looking for handouts. During one diner visit, he ate the bread crust from Mom's French Dip sandwich, prompting a quick question to the restaurant owners from Mom and a drive back home with the cat, no question whether to keep him.

In my visits home from college, I watched the cat Mom named Cinder and I nicknamed Black Bear explore the woods of our backyard, sometimes following like a dog on a trail reaching across a bridge and up the mountain. His territorial needs were a smaller-scale version of a mountain lion's, which required between fifty to a hundred and fifty square miles for males, and about half this area for females. Black Bear would scratch on a wooden bear my mom had placed on the bank in back of the house, marking this boundary between the yard and the forest just as a larger cat might, the scratches he left on the evolving landscape no less enduring. Squak Mountain State Park had grown from the Bullitt family's 600 donated acres to 1,500 acres in state parkland, an additional 1,000 acres of county land allocated for wildlife of all kinds.

In Mom's vegetable garden, Black Bear divided his time between hunting small rodents and rolling in the dirt, sometimes accepting my out-stretched hand, other times stomping away from it.

"He's a busy cat," Mom explained, apologizing for him. The bell he wore on his daytime collar jingled in rhythm to his even strides, the sound warning birds and tempering his reach. Although domestic cats were safer indoors from dogs, cars, and disease, our newest cat had trouble adjusting, never forgetting life in the trees, the collar a compromise. Mom resumed garden digging of her own, able to read the soil as easily as she did a book, well versed in the sunlight's reach and the oversized toad living in a burrow at the garden's edge. She looked away from Black Bear, not needing to see him to understand him, as torn between indoors and out as he was.

On a day filled with early autumn clouds and the irony of a mountain lion closer to downtown Seattle than the Douglas fir stretching toward the mountaintop outside, I spread pages of the *Issaquah Press* across the table, on the hunt for big cat news, trying to understand the terrain we shared. The *Press* was a weekly paper, the only one Dad subscribed to.

"It's more likely to be in the daily paper," Dad reminded me.

Through online news and the newspaper I bought in town, I learned the reactions of Seattle residents who'd seen the mountain lion in Discovery Park since late August. On their way down forested driveways to set out the trash they'd spot his golden-eyed stare. Walks through the park revealed a long, curved tail unlike any dog, a sight not easily clarified or explained. Despite the big cat's need for miles of space, everyone wondered how he'd ventured so close to the city.

Fish and Wildlife personnel like Nicholas Jorg speculated the cat, traveling at night, had lost his bearings and wandered into territory more urban than he'd intended. The most likely scenario placed him in one of the area's recent storms, every pair of blinding car lights sending the cat closer to city boundaries and farther from the familiar territory he sought. I imagined neighbors' faces when they spotted a bigger cat than expected, the competing thrill and bewilderment of discovering a housecat several times the size it was supposed to be.

"Have you ever seen a mountain lion?" I asked Dad.

He shook his head. "I saw a bobcat a few years ago, up on the bank." He described its prowl along a fallen log lined with underbrush, an outline visible only for a few strides before disappearing into the trees and the thicker forest lining the mountain.

On the bank outside, the same corridor where Dad spotted the bobcat, a carved cedar bear bore the nine-inch high scratches of Black Bear, a smaller version of the three-foot marks a bobcat would make or the impressive six-foot marks of the mountain lion. Black Bear shared the illusiveness of his larger cousins, hiding in raspberry vines or sleeping under a sword fern in the bark mulch Dad spread to discourage weeds.

Only Mom seemed unsurprised when the cat emerged without warning from one of Dad's scotch broom or from her own thick tangle of strawberry plants in the sunniest part of the garden, where he'd been watching us all along. She coaxed him inside at night, taking off the collar and its bell after sunset so he wouldn't turn into prey.

My dad looked out the window, as if the bobcat he'd seen was still there. "I grabbed the camera to take a few pictures of the bobcat," Dad said. "I didn't know whether I had film in the camera or not."

I took my own picture of Dad at the threshold in his socks, camera pointed from the warmth of the house to the rain outside, still a few years before digital cameras became the norm. During the next part of the story, illusive as the mountain lion in Discovery Park or as Black Bear prowling the garden, Dad would share the photos he'd taken of this bobcat captured on a path between domestic and wild before it faded back into the forest.

"Turns out, there wasn't any film," Dad said, waiting a moment to let the glimpse he'd failed to record in any permanent way sink in. "I opened the camera, and it was empty."

On September 6, the Discovery Park mountain lion heard dogs. He blended into the brush without a single broken branch or rustled leaf, just as he'd done before to escape unwanted encounters. He climbed a tree housecat-style, high enough to escape a human's stare or a dog's lip-curled snarl. It was the first time Jorg, the wildlife officer who'd trailed the big cat through the park, had actually seen him. The officer aimed a tranquilizer gun in the cat's direction, sedating the mountain lion with a quick shot and no lasting harm.

That day's television newscasts and the next day's newspapers showed the mountain lion collared like Black Bear and half-conscious, eyes closed like a kitten and slumbering on a bed of ferns in his transport container. The GPS collar he wore would track his future in a more distant forest. Wildlife personnel drove him from the urban territory he'd prowled in Discovery Park to a rural area northeast of Seattle. Television footage showed the mountain cat loping away, long tail bent up in a "C." A ranger and dogs followed close behind, their shouts and barks an unpleasant association for the mountain lion to remember and avoid in future wanderings.

Around the same time, in another suburban community, a mountain lion skirted the city with less good fortune. A young male, chasing new territory or turned around by the weather, was struck by a car and killed on a freeway in Redmond, east of Seattle.

Appearances of big cats in urban areas prompted some area residents to express safety concerns, even lifting of a hunting ban. Other viewpoints centered on dwindling territory for the big cats given the area's rapid growth, prompting these wide-ranging animals closer to humans, intersections inevitable. Stress and change likewise played a role in these unusual wanderings. Facing altered territory or a shifting climate, any sudden change in circumstance, many big cats acted in unusual ways, similar to their housecat cousins.

Years ago, Black Bear investigated the house I'd grown up in with extra care, padding amidst the funeral commotion of guests, baked goods, and boxes of assorted shoes. The other cats and I sat in the background while neighbors rearranged Mom's many animal figurines in preparation for a gathering in her honor. Six years after I moved to Texas, Mom, then 68, died of a sudden heart attack, something none of us, least of all her, saw coming. Scheduled for a visit home later in July, I moved my reservation up two weeks early, flying on Fourth of July night—a holiday she'd loved—over tiny flashes of light, distant celebrations far removed.

After the funeral and the gathering at Dad's, I portioned wet cat food and topped it with leftover scraps. Black Bear and our other cats, Muppet, Binky, and Fritz, reappeared after the commotion one at a time, drawn by the smell of food and a history of enough for all. Just as several cats living in close proximity work out their differences through subtle claims of scent or perching on desirable furniture, a missing household member creates a similar flux and uncertain territory to navigate.

Dad, Ken, and I wandered the house as the cats did, relearning our roles with one another in the absence of Mom. My visits to the Northwest and the blue-curtained room where I slept grew more frequent, visiting Dad and Ken and letting this new version of home sink in. Most trips, Black Bear humored me by curling at my feet atop the covers. By morning, he'd mew at my door to meet the first dew outside. The dark cat with a discrete purr came and went as he pleased just as Mom had, torn between the safety of a kitchen warmed by a wood stove and the lure of the changeable landscape outside, beyond reach of assurances.

Around the time of the Discovery Park mountain lion, Dad's neighbors found a deer carcass on a main road leading to his house. Soon after, another neighbor sighted a mountain lion in the trees close to the deer remains. Both mountain cat and deer carcass appeared in the woods between two school bus stops, one the red building at the top of the cul-de-sac where I used to catch the bus, the other on the corner down the road, my backup site if I missed the bus the first time. Now, I saw this childhood route in a different light, strides of a mountain cat overlapping the ones I'd made years before.

The closest John and I had come to a mountain lion was my hometown's Cougar Mountain Zoo, a sanctuary for animals fallen on hard times. Some had been kept as pets, while others were orphaned or injured in the wild, preventing them from returning to it. In one of the zoo's big cat enclosures, mountain lions Merlin and Nashidoitsa (Nashi) shared an outdoor space with room to climb, prowl, and nap. Nashi, whose name was Blackfoot for "Spirit of the Mountains," was discovered as an abandoned kitten in Minnesota, the only known mountain lion to come from this area in recent history. Merlin, also orphaned, was found in California and brought to the zoo as a kitten. Nashi searched for the meat strewn throughout the enclosure in unhurried stealth, reminding me of Black Bear's prowls, the soft wind chime of his bell.

Nashi and Merlin weren't the only examples of big cats living in urban terrain, particularly as cities stretched to meet areas where wildlife prowled. The mountain lion population of Washington State in 2015 was estimated at two thousand, not an overwhelming number. Nonetheless, in 2008 the Washington State Department of Wildlife had predicted a likelihood of additional encounters given the combination of increasing human population and decreasing mountain lion habitat.

When I flew up for a trip home during a December storm, the first Christmas after Mom died, Black Bear stayed inside more than usual, the failed electricity and winter ice all the coaxing he needed to sleep near the wood stove. I let him have the armchair closest to the wood stove, taking the small footstool for myself and giving him his distance. At first the house was decoration-free, none of us feeling festive, but I decided my holiday-loving mom wouldn't have endorsed such a dreary version of Christmas. Dad bought a tree, and I pulled up boxes of decorations from downstairs, not the happiest of holidays but a new normal to learn.

In the years to come, Black Bear outlived Mom's other indoor cats. He would lounge in the bedroom on top of Dad's open history books or inspect the forest perimeter like Mom used to. While wildlife crowded closer on the mountain, Black Bear kept his outdoor vigil close, peering from ferns on the rare moments I discovered him outside or emerging at the small sliding window above the kitchen sink on warm summer days, an option left open for him.

Dad called me the night we lost Black Bear. Something killed him out front, probably a coyote, he said. I was in my early thirties, and a few years had passed since Mom died. I didn't know what to say at first, the ache of losing not only the cat but a link to Mom.

Dad paused. "I should've left the outdoor light on."

"I'm sure it wouldn't have mattered." I shook my head though Dad couldn't see me, remembering how much the cat and Mom loved the forested yard, the sanctuary they'd both found in this corridor of in-betweens.

On the last day of my September visit, Ken and I took advantage of eighty-degree weather to hike up two-thousand-foot Squak Mountain, the flatter peak between the two mountains named for cats, Tiger Mountain and Cougar Mountain. Ken chose a different path than usual, a steep, direct route in the trees. Despite the weather, the trail was quiet, our only companions a hiker or two and warmth-lulled songbirds that hadn't yet migrated. The morning turned to noon, the sun overhead and the wrong time of day to see wildlife, although I thought about the most recent mountain lion Dad had mentioned by the bus stop, imagining it watching us behind old-growth stumps mixed with second-growth Douglas fir. The wildlife came closer now, flowers of Mom's backyard trimmed by deer and coyote visits more frequent, mountain lions passing through boundaries we'd constructed.

Up the road and past the last stands of Douglas fir, hemlock, and cedar, Ken and I reached the summit's radio towers, the sky clear yet thick, leafy alders shading the view. Through the early twentieth century, miners searched the mountainsides for coal, while loggers cut most of its old growth forest. Similar to the wildlife, plant life was now reclaiming the mountain, regenerating itself in canopies and fallen logs.

Ken and I chose another trail for our trip back, a sunny avenue closer to a creek thinned to a late-summer trickle and lined by deciduous trees. From the ample brush along the trail, it looked as if no one had passed this way in weeks. Ken pointed to a huge hemlock on the hillside, telling me it looked like old growth and a sign of what this forest would one day become given its protected status, wilderness within reach of the metropolitan Seattle area.

Though the broad trunk Ken pointed at showed no sign of deep-set claw marks, the kind leaving bark intact, it didn't mean the big cats weren't around, brushing up against inhabited landscapes like the Discovery Park mountain lion. I was almost glad we didn't spot any big cats, not only for our own safety but also because their invisibility meant they could still be wild here.

A few months after our hike, a neighbor spotted a mountain lion slipping through my dad's backyard and close to the fallen log above the rock wall, the same place the bobcat and Black Bear roamed in this backyard wildlife corridor. Dad believed the story just as much as if he'd seen the cat himself. "You'd have to be looking out the window at just the right time to see him," Dad said. "A glance away, and he'd be gone."

On the sliding door in the kitchen, the one Black Bear used to sit in front of until we made out his green eyes shining in the dusk and let him in, long raccoon fingers made gray prints against the glass, a reminder it was their home too. Though Mom's cats were long gone, the big cats maintained their presence here with a Seattle capture, a sighting in Dad's neighborhood, and a backyard glimpse.

I walked the route the mountain lion had followed, up the bank and behind the rock wall beside a log taken more each year by moss. Mom's wooden bear kept its vigil, Black Bear's marks revealing old claims. No mountain lion tracks tempted me, though the big cat's favorite prey, deer, left a calling card of scat in careful piles. Ferns stilled from the wind holding its breath behind the clouds. This sighting on the mountain was a thirdhand story yet inevitable, footfalls coming back in quiet strides to meet us.

10

MOUNTAIN MEADOWS

During a late summer visit, I sat up at Dad's house in the middle of the night, the mountain outside dark. I shook my head, groggy after only a few hours' sleep. Even Dad, a night owl in retirement, had long since gone to bed. Sounds of the fridge opening and footsteps on a wood floor came from the kitchen, meaning my brother was up and awake, too. I left John, his eyes and ears closed to my stumbling and not-so-quiet search for socks, jeans, and a t-shirt. With the dent in my pillow still fresh, I grabbed a fleece, a water bottle, and the Mount Rainier guidebook my brother had given me for Christmas. Ken's twenty-five-year-old Honda waited outside, parked and purring in the driveway. At 2 a.m., Ken and I left the house to meet the mountain at dawn, a two-hour drive for me to process Dad's news from the night before.

From the house on Squak Mountain, whether hidden by clouds or shining against a blue background, Mount Rainier loomed close, as if someone had painted a picture and hung it in the sky. The mountain's smooth sides appeared between stands of neighboring Douglas fir, sometimes with a crown of clouds on top. Other times, the clouds hid its base, making it look as though the mountain were floating. Viewing it wasn't an everyday occurrence. Mount Rainier emerged only on the clearest of days, as if it didn't want anyone taking it for granted, lulling viewers into an unlikely permanence.

Because Dad lived further south and closer to Mount Rainier, Ken often left from Squak Mountain as a starting point—traveling in the middle of the night ensured he'd have a mix of solitude with perfect morning light. An even bigger advantage on this particular trip was a forecast of clear skies, something never easy to predict and even less certain for a mountain reaching deep into the clouds.

An active volcano and part of the Pacific Ring of Fire, Mount Rainier, at around half a million years old, is one of the youngest peaks in the Cascade Mountain range—surrounding peaks are millions of years older. Formed by repeated lava flows and eruptions over time, Mount Rainier towers roughly three miles above the Northwest lowlands. One pivotal event shaping the mountain took place 5,600 years ago following a period of eruptions and a subsequent avalanche. During this cataclysmic event, a wall of mud, the Osceola Mudflow, traveled down the valley floor to what is now the community of Enumclaw (EE-num-claw). The mudflow would be one of many stormy alterations on the mountain, first named Tahoma or Takhoma by Native Americans.

Ken drove his Honda Accord through towns with Native American origin such as Puyallup (pyoo-AL-up), a town west of Enumclaw. At this late hour, with no other cars in sight, soft streetlights lit our way. Though it was late summertime in the Northwest, the air chilled between night and dawn. I tightened my seatbelt over the fleece I'd pulled on, fighting to stay awake. The night before, Dad had told me I could share his news with Ken, though I didn't know how and wasn't sure I should. It'd be best heard from Dad, I reasoned, slipping back into silence. The road tightened between rows of trees, and although we couldn't see it yet in the black-purple light, the mountain grew closer.

The road started climbing after that, a gradual ascent over switchbacks against the mountainsides. Our drive transitioned from a roadway hidden in the trees to a viewpoint where the woods parted, showing only darkness for now. The road ended in a hotel and information center perched on the side of a hill. At Paradise, one of Mount Rainier's most popular areas, we parked next to a few other cars, most of them probably belonging to employees. Formed in 1899 and the fifth of America's national parks, Mount Rainier National Park receives close to two million visitors each year to camp, hike, and explore the 369-square-mile area of forests and vistas. The park stays open most of the year, although certain parts are closed for winter—Paradise, center of winter activities in the park, receives around 640 inches of snow each year.

I looked up at the mountain, still a white suggestion in the sky. Considered a training ground for Mount Everest, around ten thousand individuals attempt to climb Mount Rainier each year, with about half of them succeeding. Visitors like us came for hiking or to admire the summer flowers close-up. At 4 a.m., the skyline at Paradise, near 5,400 feet, brightened fields of ice and snow layered above us. The most glaciated peak in the United States, Mount Rainier's slopes offered a more turbulent past than its pastel-covered slopes suggested.

The US Geological Survey describes the most recent large landslide on Mount Rainier as a five-hundred-year-old volcanic mudslide, or *lahar,* hurtling down the volcano's west side and the start of the Puyallup River. Termed "the Electron Mudflow," numerous residences and farms now sit atop it, marking one of the main changes to impact this mountain—communities growing up close around it.

Carrying Ken's tripod and camera gear, we set off on the trails, the mountain's dark outline shadowing us. I moved my feet with careful steps, eyes searching the ground yet drawn to the purple giant hovering above us. Dad's news was a change for the better, I reasoned. It'd been seven years since Mom died, ample time for him to start a new life. Opening my mouth to tell Ken, I breathed out the clear, thin altitude instead.

Ken stopped at a point in the trail he'd visited before, an alpine meadow promising layers of blue lupine and Indian paintbrush. It was still too dark to take pictures, the mountain suggested yet not fully revealed. I sat on a flat rock and hugged my arms. Ken set up his tripod, his movements slow and deliberate, willing to wait for the mountain. Surrounded by the cold and no longer warmed by our walk, I pulled my sleeves down until they covered my wrists and browsed the slick guidebook, unable to decipher its trails in the predawn light.

Ken kept his face against the camera lens and aimed, the only hunting he cared for. He set the tripod on several rocky spots along the trail before finding one he liked, setting his equipment bags nearby. I kept my perch on the cold rock opposite the trail and thought about the news he'd hear later that day, the shifting landscape of home.

Mount Rainier's last major event took place between 1820 and 1894, with fourteen eruptions, some of which may have been dust clouds rising from falling rock. Although the mountain has kept a silent countenance ever since, seismic activity indicates it could become active in the future with eruptions similar to or even larger than those of the past. Melting snow and ice will have the potential to pick up loose rock and mud to form lahars, taking everything and everyone in their path.

Another visitor came into view in the dim light, a man crouching off the trail as if he were hiding. Ken pointed out equipment similar to his own, a few camera bags and a tripod. The shots the man aimed for, in the middle of a burst of flowers, would prove dramatic, but at a price. The fields of Paradise, which once held ski rope tows, tent camping, and a golf course, have since been cleared of these activities, with a renewed focus on preserving the subalpine meadows. Signs throughout the park urged visitors to stay on the trail and not disturb the terrain, including its robust though short-lived flowers blooming from mid-July to mid-September.

Ken and I stayed where we were, preparing for the mountain to emerge. Years before, we'd driven to eastern Washington on a Sunday night to view a total solar eclipse first thing in the morning. On the other side of the mountains, a necessity for clear skies, we'd listened to the collective sigh of onlookers on barren hillsides when the sky turned pastel, an instant sunset. On the cardboard pieces I'd brought to project the image, the moon consumed the first chunk of sun until the whole star disappeared, all except rays streaming outside the edges, birds quiet and the air chilled for minutes that felt more final than temporary. While a few people shrieked from fear or excitement, Ken and I kept silent, waiting for the sun to come back to life from behind the moon, the hillside made new again.

First light glowed around Mount Rainier, turning it pink, the stars behind it disappearing. My rock warmed and the flowers at our feet came into view, purple-blue and crimson to match the sky. It was easy to sit here now, watching the flowers explode on either side of the trail around us in their early August peak. My brother moved his camera with ease, capturing the mountain in full flower before the light, the weather, or some other circumstance modified this particular moment into something else altogether.

After an hour of shots, Ken packed his gear into a waiting backpack. I tied my shoes, collected my guidebook, and stretched my legs on the now-sunny rock. Ken led me to one of the trails he liked best, the Skyline Trail, other footprints revealing its popularity. The path was dry and strewn with small rocks compared to the lush multicolored meadow we'd just visited, the midmorning sun burning colors away. Although we skirted the mountain rather than heading straight up, the climb steepened. I watched my brother's assured footsteps a stride ahead of mine. The news from last night, for now, stayed unmentioned.

The trail ended in a small platform of rock and the reward of a mountain peak in every direction—Mount Adams, Mount St. Helens, and Mount Hood. I turned in a circle to capture each purple-white summit. Their solidity gave these volcanoes a lasting appearance, although they were subject to uneven forces beneath them, tectonic plates poised atop one another. Even the park website reminded visitors of Mount Rainier's dynamic countenance, an active volcano with the potential for great harm. While many believe danger would keep its distance, the park website cautions "only you can decide if you want to spend time in this unpredictable and changing landscape."

We hiked a few other trails before a lack of sleep and food caught up with me, taking me back to the car to wait for Ken, who'd set out to explore a closer, forested summit. In the afternoon, we drove back to Dad's house on streets that had come to life in summer heat. Saturday traffic, so absent in our morning drive, now crowded narrow freeway lanes, a contrast to the empty streets we'd driven on that morning. In the car's growing heat with no AC to ease it, I wondered if I should tell my brother ahead of time, if it'd soften the news a little. I drifted back to noncommittal sleep instead, waking up too late to say anything when the car crunched over driveway gravel toward the house we'd grown up in.

Inside, I fiddled with the snack drawer as if I still lived there and handed a candy bar to John. My pulled-back hair was straight and sticky from hiking. Ken's hair reacted just like John's, curling in thick waves. Dad and Karyl joined us in the kitchen. Ken had met Karyl before, I reasoned. She was tall, like Dad, and shared his sense of humor. The news would surprise Ken less.

"Karyl and I are getting married," Dad said.

Ken sat down when he heard the news—like me, it was the first time he'd met her. I turned to the picture window in the kitchen, the one overlooking the deck. Mount Rainier, the mountain we'd just visited, glowed periwinkle in the late summer sky. The mountain looked the same as it had on sunny afternoons for years, although I knew it, too, faced slow changes over time.

At Christmas, John and I returned to the house on Squak Mountain. A small Douglas fir waited outside the house for us to bring inside. "Your dad said you like to decorate the tree," Karyl said. She'd left Mom's paintings of barns, the glass cats, and copper pots. We talked in the kitchen, Dad sitting close to Karyl, his fingers entwined with hers. From Dad's house, Mount Rainier showed off its angular top despite a few trees growing around the edges of what we could see.

Ken took me to another place to view the mountain from the side of Squak Mountain, a trail I'd never been on. On the cloudless day Ken chose, we came to a spot on the edge of the state land and a clearing you had to know about to find. In the sparse foliage of early fall, Mount Rainier filled the sky close enough to touch, the valley spread out below like a lap. The assuredness of this landmark belied its changeability.

Although the climate at home steadied after our morning on Rainier, this changed months later, once we learned Karyl had cancer. Short of two years into their marriage, hospice workers arrived with a diet of medication and soft words. I sat near Karyl's bed by the picture window and watched the rain while she slept between visitors. Sick as she was, I caught glimpses of the woman whose banter made Dad smile, an expression frequent as Mount Rainier on clear-skied, late summer days.

In 2006, a storm came, not a volcanic eruption, but an outbreak of wind and rain. Eighteen inches of precipitation unleashed against Mount Rainier in ground already saturated by rain and snow, causing the worst flooding of the park's 108-year history. The storm destroyed roads and campsites and changed the course of rivers. The Nisqually River flooded five acres of land at Sunshine Point and damaged several roadways within the park. The storm also impacted many of the park's low-lying trails. At Paradise, where Ken and I began our hike, the water reservoir filled with mud and debris. Following the storm, freezing weather burst a pipe in Paradise Inn, causing extensive water damage.

The weather turned cold for Karyl's funeral, even though it was early April. Dad said it wasn't necessary for us to fly back from Austin, although John and I, both living in West Texas, didn't listen. Having lost one parent nine years ago, I thought I'd bring a more assured grasp of how to act or what to say, but the terrain proved no easier in my early forties, the footing no steadier.

After the church service on Squak Mountain, tree branches wavered with uncertainty. It was supposed to rain, though sunshine broke through in patches. The church for Karyl's funeral service perched on the same side of the foothill as Mom's gravesite.

"Look inside the church and see if anything's left," Dad said after the funeral service. Wearing a charcoal-colored suit, he made his way to the Trooper, driving home so people could follow him to the reception he was hosting. After double-checking we'd picked up everything, Ken, John, and I walked past the shrieks of children in the church playground. A group of them dressed in navy uniforms rushed by with their soccer ball, oblivious to the funeral and its somber blacks and grays.

At the door to Karyl's silver sedan, I waited before stepping into the driver's seat, not ready to leave this side of the mountain for Dad's house just yet. The top of Squak Mountain curved above us, green and flat-topped compared to formidable Mount Rainier yet no less subject to change and loss.

"Let's go see Mom first," I said.

Ken hesitated, a moment before answering "sure."

John, in the front seat beside me, nodded. "We'd better make it fast, though." Instead of joining the line of cars curving down the valley road to Dad's house, we followed a twisting route uphill. My heart raced faster than I drove, though I reminded myself there was time for this stop on the other side of the mountain from Dad's place—Karyl wouldn't mind.

Over time, Mount Rainier recovered from the cataclysmic flood that changed the course of rivers, trails, and campsites and closed the park for half a year. Road crews rebuilt the Sunshine Point road, including a utility line, with ten thousand tons of rock helping to secure the road and protect it from the Nisqually River. Workers restored park trails and other amenities, from reinforcing roadways to rebuilding hiking trails. Along with installing culverts to facilitate the Kautz Creek's new direction, crews restored power to both Longmire and Paradise. Coping with the area's typical heavy snowfall, crews dug out the reservoir and continued with renovations planned at Paradise. In 2008, a new Paradise Inn and Paradise Visitor Center opened for guests.

Ken, John, and I parked at the edge of the Hillside Cemetery, filled with early grass and pink flowers visitors had placed. I arranged the lilacs I'd picked from Dad's house while John stood close, Ken setting his palm on the black granite stone. Back in Karyl's sedan, we drove down the valley and up the other side of Squak Mountain where white-starred trilliums returned despite the weather, Mount Rainier in view along the way.

11
The Voice of Wood

Between rain-green foothills on Highway 101, a tugboat listed upward, landlocked in a grassy wave. I stared at this roadside distraction in our search for wood, a day-trip John suggested during a visit with my dad. John's eyes stayed fixed on the road, trusting my description of the beached boat without looking. Along with the musical instruments John repaired at work and a 1920s Jusak bass he was restoring, John dreamed of shaping bass instruments from wood still smelling of moss and rain.

While I shaped sentences to fit essays, John heard musical tones in concentric circles of wood, each year layered in more than one kind of pitch. As a luthier, he repaired cellos, upright basses, and violins, reviving the cracked, bent, and broken. In a throwaway, upgrade-now culture, his profession's perspective stretched longer, a marriage of everyday adjustments and faith in the unknown.

Little changed from the 1600s, the luthier profession remained an art of curved wood, hot liquids, and taut bow hair, all resulting in stringed instruments with the strength of an egg yet vulnerable to cracks and serious breaks. Becoming a luthier took attention to detail and steadiness, a hundred bows restrung to gain a foothold, liters of turpentine-smelling varnish mixed to achieve the desired color and consistency.

The twenty-year-old Isuzu Trooper we drove, my dad's car, rumbled through the June rain on four slow-powered cylinders and scant mileage at 37,000 miles. For buyers and sellers of the aged wood we sought, the outlook proved just as long term. Many sellers repurposed trees from fallen stands or from logs used as fishing piers. It would take an additional five years or more for the wood to dry from its time in saltwater or life of mountain rain. Buyers of this wood, meanwhile, required the dedication to plane and carve, smooth and sand, taking their time until they reached the instrument inside a fallen tree or discarded wood scrap. In seeking wood to repurpose, John created new ties to the region, making the most of our visits here.

I fiddled with the map of the peninsula until it slipped out of my hands and fell onto the car floor. Plenty of farms filled this landscape, yet nothing stood out as a wood mill. Lulled by the green scenery, I wasn't sure we'd find the Wood Well, which so far escaped both our eyes and GPS. While I was open to distractions like a tugboat on a hillside, John's outlook on the goal proved steadier. He pulled over and reached for the paper map on the floor.

"Does your phone have a signal?" he asked, more prepared to ask for directions than I'd been.

I started to shape the word *no*—it was too remote on this corner of Olympic Peninsula forty miles and a ferry ride from my hometown on the mainland. Before I could say anything, a few bars appeared on the screen, enough to make a call. I punched in the number scrawled on the map bottom and described the turnout we were parked in.

"Look for the tugboat in the front yard," a woman's voice on the other end said with practiced calm. "You can't miss it."

John turned the car back toward the tugboat and outbuildings we'd drifted past a minute ago. After parking the Trooper by one of the barns, we dodged puddles and followed the fresh tree scent inside. Cut wood stacked like books filled the shelves from floor to ceiling. Each piece in this library contained whorls and filigree, a calligraphy John read as pure potential.

Jamie, the woman I'd talked with on the phone, stepped outside the office, a warm corner section of the building. "Can I help you?"

"I'm looking for corner blocks," John said. Small spruce blocks, a first step in the bass John planned to build, reinforced the inside of the instrument and provided its foundation.

Blonde hair tucked tight into her collar, Jamie told us Matt, their expert on wood for stringed instruments, had the day off. She gave us a tour of the wood instead, showing us shelves of violin-sized pieces.

A barn across the driveway held larger pieces of stacked wood along with powerful saws, which for now stood silent. We followed Jamie up a narrow set of stairs to a plywood attic floor and the largest wood pieces leaning against a back wall. Their position several layers back hinted at how long they'd been resting there, a good sign. John examined pieces of rectangular spruce large enough to build a bass top. Prized for its ability to hold string pressure, spruce was light enough to transfer vibrations, or the voice of a bass. Paired with a maple back and sides for strength, the marriage of woods gave the instrument a solid foundation.

John turned back downstairs with slow steps, reluctant to leave the possibilities he'd seen in careful rows. In a driveway between the two buildings, another Wood Well employee, a man with a gray-peppered beard, took over from Jamie and led us across Highway 101 to search for corner blocks. The clouds dipped close, a line of smoke trailing from a nearby house the only sign of warmth. Inside a shed perched on the hillside, the bearded man showed us three-foot logs stacked floor to ceiling like firewood. "Can you work with one of these?" he asked.

John nodded and placed a few logs the man handed him into the Trooper. They weren't so large we couldn't take one or two back to Austin on the plane, a step toward the bass he'd create. "How much do I owe you?"

The man, heading toward one of the hillside houses in the gray afternoon light, shook his head. "No charge," he said. "Come back and see us."

After closing time in the Austin violin shop where John worked, fluorescent lamp glow replaced daylight. The Jusak bass, John's restoration project, covered a workbench in the middle of the room. Like John, it split its time between home and work, depending on the task, the tools, and where we had space.

Luthier work took specialized training. For John, it meant a move to Redwing, Minnesota, and a yearlong immersion in school, while I finished a writing degree in West Texas. Because we'd lived apart my first year away—John stayed in Austin while I lived in Lubbock—we were ready for long-distance life with family-plan cell phones and dish sets in pairs. We hoarded frequent flyer miles and saw each other every few weeks, in the West Texas landscape I'd discovered or his adopted Midwest, each of us taking artistic and economic leaps of faith. In the weeks before graduation, we decided to live where the first job pointed us. Blackerby Violin, a violin shop in Austin, hired John almost immediately. The 1950s house we'd leased to other students waited for us.

I sat on a stool to record John's progress and separate craft from mystery. The liquid he stirred on a double burner bubbled like a potion, with violins floating from unseen wires overhead. Each instrument contained a paper ticket slipped between its strings with a wish list for John to fulfill, anything from strings and bridge setup to more complex fixes of body and finish. I imagined the customers who'd visited the workshop that day—school-age students with instructors peering over John's shoulder to catch the small adjustments he made or professional musicians admiring the Jusak.

John discovered the bass online at a violin shop in Mystic, Connecticut. The owner of the shop was candid about this fixer-upper. "The bass needs a lot of work," he said on the phone. "It has cracks in the bottom, sides, and a substantial one in the neck."

"I can do the repairs myself," John said. It didn't matter he couldn't see the bass, much less play it. The Jusak, of German and Czech origins, was a possibility he could hear.

Although not as well-known as Italian builders, German makers had established their own history of instrument building. Southern Germany in particular supplied much of this woodworking expertise, with makers such as Jacob Stainer, a seventeenth-century master builder who had a gift for selecting wood.

"What happens if you don't like how it sounds?" I asked, unsure.

"I'll sell it," John said, though I could tell this wasn't his first instinct. As with any good relationship, he wanted to give his best.

After watching John take off the bass top several months ago, I'd helped him replace it, a job requiring the same water-soluble glue he now cooked and a set of clamps lining the bass sides. Inside the bass, John had fused small cracks using strips of linen for the curved parts of the bass and slips of wood shaped like diamonds to bind flatter portions. In making all the Jusak repairs himself, John followed an example set by Italian violin-maker Stradivarius, who partnered each luthier with a single bass.

John walked across the violin shop holding a new bass neck he'd cut and carved from a piece of maple. Because of the size and placement of the crack in the original bass neck, it'd been a safer investment to replace it than repair it. "The neck represents forty percent of the instrument's weight," he said, showing me the fingerboard made of ebony he'd glue on top of it.

As a trial run, John fitted the new neck into the shoulder of the bass. The two slipped into one another as if they were one, a good sign, although this close fit meant John had to pound the wood with a mallet to break the pieces apart in preparation for a more permanent connection. The glue, no longer boiling, simmered on the nearby burner. Using a hairdryer, he warmed the wood so the glue would set slower. With a broad paintbrush, John painted the watery glue on the neck and shoulder, bonding them into the long-term. Each step revealed measured yet even progress, much like the workshop growing in our own backyard.

* * *

In a workspace lined with rows of tools and violin posters, John mixed wine-colored syrup, a new varnish. The Jusak rested on a "spit" designed to hold the bass at either end, its sides touching nothing but air.

Oak branches rustled outside the workshop we'd built over the summer. After debating affordable improvements to our bungalow home, we compromised on the shop, a structure complementing the house without overpowering our narrow, bowling alley-shaped yard. John painted blue walls outside lined in white trim to match the clouds.

I returned to South Austin after living in West Texas with new landscapes to describe, boxes of books, and Mitzi, the rescue cat we'd adopted in Lubbock. After John removed the Jusak top, Mitzi began sleeping inside the bass. She napped for hours on what might have been a bed of moon wood, trees harvested from the Carpathian Forest during a full-moon cycle. Luthier tradition claimed this wood contained special properties, such as extra stability.

John returned from school in Redwing, Minnesota, with a broadened expanse of tools, the most tangible a knife, carved smooth from figured maple. He brought back figurative tools as well. Already a musician, woodworker, and artisan, he became an alchemist in the Midwest, stirring concoctions designed to fuse and last.

A varnish recipe warmed on a hot plate. Bottles of spirit varnish, named for its alcohol base, lined a shelf, all of them dark and lettered in all-caps so no one mistook them for potent wine. I grew used to these unusual brews, a few of them finding their way inside the house and on top of our refrigerator.

Although I anticipated the varnish would be syrup-thick, the resulting liquid was light in color and consistency. It would take over a month and five patient coats of varying shades for John to achieve the result he wanted, a golden brown reminiscent of the original bass color. At some unseen signal, John dipped a brush into the quick-drying varnish and worked fast to coat the bass, his brush whispering against the wood sides.

After he covered the sides, top, and bottom, John grasped the bass by the neck and moved it to a space that could pass for a closet, but in reality was a light box inspired by a mentor, James Ham, whom we'd visited in Victoria, Canada. Like James, John outfitted a space with fluorescent lights to dry the instrument. With each coat, the bass rested in intense light behind a closed door with taped edges, not revealing the transition within.

Between working at Blackerby, playing weekend gigs, and stoking our own home fires, restoring the Jusak would take John a year to complete, making the day he took the bass inside our house to set it up with strings and a bridge almost secondary to its restoration. With no announcement, John plucked the four wide strings. There was much at stake. I stayed fixed to the words on my computer without reading them, holding my breath and listening. The aged wood's pure tone shared a better than hoped for result, each note more beginning than end.

In an unhurried trip from Edmonds to our destination of Quilcene, Washington, green waves splashed against the ferryboat. I climbed the stairs to the observation deck with John and waited for land. We knew where we were headed this time, to a business tucked between the Olympic Mountains and a tugboat sailing against a hillside. Months ago, we admired violin-sized slabs covered in ornate grain along with larger pieces, anticipating the day John would buy additional wood to create a bass from scratch.

Back in our car and following the careful line of cars off the ferry, I called Aunt Delores, who lived on the southern end of the peninsula in Shelton. We'd visit her in an hour as part of a circular trip John named "round the sound." Rain spit up between the tires while the air outside chilled. A December storm dumped a foot and a half of snow, unusual for both its intensity and early appearance. Now, the wind blew a more temperate yet unsettled wind, Douglas fir branches waving their fringed arms above us along the way.

John pointed the car west on Highway 104, heading for the coastline. After our discovery last spring, the Wood Well was easier to find, 104 meeting Highway 101 to run south along the Salish Sea. A few bare patches on the hillsides represented trees harvested for lumber, with young saplings replacing them. I wondered about trees felled for their voices—the whole tree was used, John assured me. If the tree wasn't repurposed from underwater service as a dock or a salmon trap, in many cases it had fallen in a windstorm, making harvest inevitable.

Arcing in a peninsula breeze, a large bird rose and swooped above us, its wings spanning several feet and lined with dark feathers. *Must be a hawk.* The bird adjusted its height for a truck barreling from the other direction and circled close above us, spiraling like the figured wood we were about to see, near enough to spot his white head and focused eye. I'd never seen a bald eagle so close, and craned my neck to keep this good omen in sight, wondering if its mate, chosen for life, rested nearby.

Once we headed south on Highway 101, foothills of the Olympic Mountains, their plump sides sugared with snow, stretched on our right-hand side. Past piles of roadside slush mixed with gravel, roadside features like our tugboat came faster.

We arrived at the Wood Well in the middle of a rain shower and hurried into the largest barn, the one with the corner office and donuts. Matt, the expert on instrument wood, met us outside the barns, telling us they once housed cattle before their current shelves full of wood for violins, cellos, and bass. I admired a wood fragment figured in graceful lines.

Protected against the elements with thick coveralls, Matt watched me study its etchings. "That's nothing." He handed me another piece, its grain covered in wild red swirls.

John looked alongside me. "It's called quilt. About one in ten trees have it."

Scientists have searched for the cause of this patterned effect—weather, water, or otherwise—with no specific conclusions reached, a mystery of why certain trees produce it and others don't.

Matt led us up a narrow staircase into the rafters containing the larger pieces of wood we'd seen last time. We walked on the plywood floor where stacks of wood, air-dried for years, rested. Only a few cryptic notes scrawled on the wall revealed the different types, yet Matt took in the wood with a quick glance, an order he'd memorized. He strode up to one of the largest pieces, a five-foot-long, three-foot-wide piece of Sitka spruce from Canada or Alaska.

John took one end and examined the length of the grain, even and red-tinged. It lacked the baroque figuring of the wood we'd just seen, a good thing. As beautiful as quilted flame was, the dense figuring also made carving more difficult. All three of us lingered on the spruce between John and Matt. John stared the longest, running his hand along the length of wood before looking at me. I nodded back.

"We'll take it," John said.

We picked our way across the plywood floor, Matt carrying the wood and John floating behind him down the narrow steps.

On the first floor, Matt stopped at a jointer, a planer designed to create flat surfaces. Matt ran the spruce piece down the entire length of the jointer, smoothing one side of the wood to a straight edge. As an extra touch, he used a smaller band saw to carve a discrete knot from the spruce corner.

Matt fired up a band saw next. From a respectable distance, the saw resembled a prop from logging days past, a blade of steel incisors running on a belt between two wheels and designed to make an even more critical cut, the one down the wood's center. From this imposing blade, two mirror-image pieces would emerge, ready for fusing down the center to create a bass top. Matt and Jamie adjusted the custom band saw to make this lengthwise cut. Minute adjustments to the saw took longer than the cutting itself, which would last only twenty seconds.

Fine sawdust outlined my hiking boots and sweetened the air. Wet and chilled as it was outside, neither John nor I said anything about returning to the warm corner office in the opposite building. After one last look at the conveyor belt the wood would rest on, Matt stepped away from the saw. Grasping the length of wood, he placed it on the belt and switched on a small motor. The saw growled to life with spinning wheels and a determined hum growing even louder and more metallic once the wood was in place. Centimeters at a time, Matt guided the spruce through the blade to Jamie on the opposite end of the saw blade, their eyes never leaving the wood.

Once the split pieces reached Jamie's side, Matt flipped off the switch, slowing the spinning wheels and rotating teeth. Holding a piece of wood in each hand, he set them down in front of us.

John saw the bass inside already. "This is where the top part will be." He traced an outline with his finger. "And here's the bottom."

I admired the twin pieces of reddish-pink wood, the bass within becoming apparent to my eyes, too. Will tapped the wood, sharing a hint of its voice to come. At John's assured knock the wood spoke louder, its clear tones a promise in the cold air.

12

BETWEEN DROUGHT AND SNOW

In a Safeway parking lot dimpled with snow, I drove Dad's sedan across ruts of ice, road stripes long gone thanks to an early winter storm. Dad and John, resigned to our crawl and slide over strip mall parking spaces filled with snowy moguls, rode without comment. Other drivers listed around us, everyone anxious to complete their errands before the next phase of this snowstorm, an unexpected holiday guest to this area.

Similar to Austin, the Seattle area wasn't built for snow, the region never receiving enough of it to justify the investment Midwest and East Coast cities made in snowplows and salt. While the main roads of the Puget Sound area were eventually cleared of this particular storm's initial four-inch snowfall, most parking lots weren't. Rather than the usual thaw a few days later, frigid temperatures froze the drifts into impromptu craters and pockmarks.

Blasting into town several days before John and I did, this early snowstorm made its debut with thunder and lightning, hallmarks of the Southwest. Once we heard about it, I told Dad we'd take the shuttle from the airport to his house on the mountain. He disagreed, telling us we were arriving between weather systems and he'd pick us up. Everyone else had the same plan, or so it seemed at the airport, both arriving and outgoing travelers crowding into this crack in the weather. At the baggage carousel, John and I took our time finding our bags and kept an eye out for Dad.

While I'd been away, the Northwest population had grown at nearly twice the North American rate—Issaquah now had traffic lights and a rush hour, along with burn bans on certain days. Like the big snow that fell the year my parents moved us into the woods, all of us impacted the area a little more each year, prompting unexpected shifts in population and weather. We realized these changes not only through cold statistics but also through anecdotal evidence, the stories we repeated to one another about warmer summers and more violent storms.

On foot, Dad, John, and I picked our way across the Safeway lot and into the dry heat of the store, its aisles thick with shoppers plotting purchases followed by quick getaways. We made our decisions faster than normal, too, not deliberating between the berry and cream pies like usual. *More snow is on the way*, Dad reminded us.

Walking back to the car, Dad aimed the shopping cart out the sliding doors and into the cold. Once its wheels met ice, the cart lurched like a sled, Dad hanging onto the back and John grasping its front. In unison and without comment, they lifted the cart, carrying it across the snow while the turkey slid off the bottom rack like a frozen football until I tackled it before a car ran it over.

The ride home wasn't much safer, though I knew what to expect this time and could even laugh a little at our grocery-filled sedan bouncing across the snow until we reached a road plowed to passable. Though the trees were frosted in ice along the way, nothing was as bad as the store lots had been.

At Dad's house, I called Ken to see if he'd join us earlier. "Maybe you'd better come sooner than later. The roads aren't too bad," I lied, "not yet." I didn't mention the parking lot as jagged as the moon or TV forecasters predicting *more snow* in monotone assuredness. If Ken, who lived an hour away, didn't make a break for it when he could, the storm would make up its mind for him. An hour later it started snowing again, scattered flakes gentle at first, thickening into a more determined descent.

As steady as the Northwest snow fell in December, the sun had burned Texas the previous summer. I watched the grass in our backyard, non-native St. Augustine, wither a blade at a time. The few strands shaded by a pecan tree were soon covered with the workshop we'd started building in the backyard, a place for John to build bass instruments. The dry weather had made the construction go faster, our contractor assured us, and I nodded, complicit in this weather shift yet still searching the sky for rain.

The summer of 2008 offered a relentless diet of 100 degree-plus days and a persistent high circling the region like a buzzard, the "H" an unchanging graphic on the evening news. Even brief escapes from the heat proved hard to come by, the drought sucking water from area lakes and melting our street to sticky tar. With the dry spell stretching from summer to fall, I missed the rain I'd experienced when I first moved to Austin, like the Northwest rain I grew up with.

John and I visited Dad for a June getaway, experiencing unseasonable cold and rain yet a welcome respite for us. In a burst of rain showers, we stopped at a fruit stand and bought boxes of blackberries and raspberries. Another customer grumbled *where'd our summer go?*

South, I wanted to say. We clutched our boxes of fruit and walked to the car, raindrops spotting the windshield. Deep in a La Niña weather pattern, precipitation in the United States had fled north, maybe to stay.

At a break in the snow showers, Ken's boots crunched up the driveway on Christmas Eve. He'd parked his car at the top of the hill in a space someone else had dug in the snowdrifts lining the unplowed road.

"Someone might have cleared that spot for themselves," Dad said.

"There was room for somebody else," Ken shrugged. Now that he'd arrived, he wasn't going anywhere, even to park. His meteorology background kept him attuned to shifts in weather—more than once, he'd suggested not living anywhere near a coastline due to predicted global rises in sea level.

"How was the drive?" I asked.

Ken shook his head. "Not good. And it's getting worse."

Weather reports promised a convergence of arctic air with moisture preparing to exhale several more inches of snow, maybe a foot or more. The last time I'd seen a snowstorm this determined was the year we'd moved to the mountain, with snow piled so high Dad could step off the roof without a ladder. Because no one bothered to plow our road back then, either, our hillside created perfect sledding after a few bold drivers packed it down.

"Too bad we don't have the sleds," Ken said. Dad had given them away to the neighbor kids years ago. My brother looked online for updated versions of our wood-and-red-metal memories; while new sleds wouldn't arrive for this particular storm, a future blizzard was likely given this uneasy weather.

Although I'd doubted their excitement, the meteorologists' reports for our current storm proved more accurate than inflammatory, as tangible as the growing pile of snow outside. Eighteen inches soon covered a picnic table on the deck while the road above our cul-de-sac disappeared. The roof of Ken's car stuck out from the top of the bank where he'd parked it, until it, too, faded into a river of white.

Twenty miles away, downtown Seattle endured similar snowy conditions, its steep side streets coated in drifts. Fearing salt would leech into and harm nearby Puget Sound, the city spread sand, police officers responding to calls on foot rather than driving on those unforgiving hills. And while the city saw less snow than elevated rural areas, this storm spread its influence with an even hand, affecting everyone.

Late in the afternoon, Dad's next-door neighbor Corinne, her black hair poking from a fleece hat and snow flying from the boots she stamped, knocked on the door. "I'm supposed to travel tonight." She shook her head, offering a box of cookies and a bottle of red wine. "I don't think I'm going to make it."

Dad was pleased with this change in plans. "You'll eat with us." He added seasoning to a pan full of steak, pepper flecking the meat until it disappeared. We opened the wine and admired the cookies, settling into housebound holidays while the storm worsened, the muffled whisper of fresh snow deepening outside.

On a Friday night in August, a hackberry tree in our Austin backyard rustled, shuddering like an animal. John walked into the yard with a flashlight and rushed back inside to unplug the computer, sprinting back outside again and yelling *it's falling* before I could do much more than leave the house and make sure John was out of the way.

He was standing too close to what was left of the tree, a four-trunked oddity split down the middle in the ten-foot space between our house and the neighbor's. By some merciful act, the four trunks, like fingers of a hand, splayed on the ground between the two houses rather than grasping either one on the way down. Thick branches covered our lawn like we'd planted new shrubs. Gutter pieces twisted with power wires, the loose lines making our house pitch black and the air conditioning unit eerie quiet. We went inside to confirm the tree hadn't pierced the plaster walls and counted ourselves lucky, even when the City of Austin told us we'd have to wait until Monday before we had power again. The neighbors' power connection, although functional, was battered—they, too, would have to live without electricity over the weekend.

Whether through age, drought, or both, our quadruple-trunked tree, the one we'd schemed with our neighbor about trimming, made up its own mind for us by cracking in two. It was the second hackberry tree we'd lost that year, the first one tumbling across our deck in a windstorm while we were visiting the Northwest in June, our access to weather in more than one place exposing extremes in sharper relief.

It was a reality we'd grow used to, an amendment from the backyards of our past and a shift described by climate change experts as adaptability. A local challenge rather than a global one, adaptability starts with an acknowledgement of the difficulties to come, an adjustment before tackling larger-scale measures in uncertain weather.

John and I slept on our deck that evening, hopeful for breezes and unwilling to abandon our dog and cat for the cool bed our neighbors offered, although we changed our minds and took them up on it the next night.

After waking up Christmas morning, John and I visited Corinne to find Ken shoveling driveway snow for her. "Merry Christmas!" Corinne said.

Drifts covered the house and garage before spilling across the yard, everything a monotone white. Partway down her sloping driveway, a parked car poked its top from the snow.

"A friend went out of town and I let her park here." Corinne sighed at the buried car.

Since the storm had arrived, we'd wrestled with it by shoveling out cars and scraping ice from the top of the cul-de-sac, our ears peeled for the roar of snowplows that never came.

News reports confirmed the urban core wasn't faring much better than the outlying areas. The tons of sand used on roadways proved ineffective in melting ice. Decisions on which roads to clear, meanwhile, drew fire from residents. Television reports showed downtown citizens in the same plight as outlying residents like us, digging out as best they could.

Corinne, older than me by a few years without looking it, broke the silence of our work with a swathe of cardboard tugged from the recycling bin and spread on the snow like a toboggan. I plopped on the cardboard, Corinne behind me. Perched at the top of the driveway, we tried to find a silver lining in the weather, to renegotiate the unpredictable. Like the buried road above our cul-de-sac, the snow defied our expectations. Despite our heels dug deep in search of traction, the paper surface inched until John grabbed an edge and pulled, flattening the cardboard against the snow until it squeaked. We made it down the driveway with enough momentum to take us past the buried car, not the ride we'd imagined, yet good enough to laugh about at the bottom.

Although the Texas drought kept its hold through fall, winter arrived in Austin with a rare shower of snowflakes dusting my round-roofed

Volkswagen Beetle. Under the young pecan tree in our front yard, I looked straight up at the snow, a galaxy of flakes destined to last only several hours on our street and layer a few inches further north. Even this small amount was enough to halt business as usual, giving me time to admire the snowman neighbor boys on the street would eventually build, its round body improvised by a basketball rolled in snow.

Our winter in the Southwest would be characterized by cooler days and falling temperatures, though little in the way of precipitation. I worried the past summer's succession of rainless days was more promise than chance. And while a few seasons of extreme weather could be attributed to variable weather patterns, researchers predict climate change will bring drought conditions to Texas more frequently in years to come.

Snow, snow, yelled another neighbor boy, the flakes an oddity for him, everyday weather becoming harder to find. Hundred-degree weeks in Austin, a foot and a half of snow in Issaquah, all of it was extreme, yet turning into business as usual, fickle weather we'd need to expect. It was the reason John and I chose a paint color called "Falling Snow" for our Austin home months later, the words more important than the hue.

At the end of our visit in the big snow, I hiked the mountain behind Dad's house with my brother, stepping into his size 13 footprints. With trail signposts long buried, we kept to the main road, a route once used for logging. Although almost every trip home included this steep climb, I'd never hiked it in two feet of snow. The muffled whiteness made it difficult to tell how far we'd come, how much farther we had to go. More than once I sat on a log saying I'd stay there and wait for Ken, whose long strides made it look easy, to go up without me. Each time I did this, he stopped, waited, and told me we were almost there, although I suspected we weren't.

A man wearing snowshoes and a snowboard pressed against his shoulder passed us part way up the mountain. I admired the optimism of this snowboarder on an otherwise deserted foothill, his ability to adapt to extreme conditions. Although the deep snow wasn't packed enough for the metal runners of a sled, a snowboard would glide over this twisting road just fine—the sheer grade of the hill would do the rest.

I breathed a quick hello to the snowboarder, my face warm and bright as the red jacket I wore. Against the mountain lengthening ahead of us, the snowboarder disappeared around the next hairpin turn.

My boots grew heavier, the ski pants I wore swishing with every step into Ken's fresh prints. Past the next few turns, the sky turned gray and the wind picked up. A Douglas fir ahead of us lost its snow in a shower of frost, fooling me into thinking it was snowing again. This moody weather matched the windy restlessness of a Texas storm, reminding me lightning could strike in cold weather, too. I walked faster and didn't suggest waiting on one of the fallen logs anymore.

"Something's moving in," Ken agreed but kept going, the summit too close to turn back.

I didn't want to turn around either, not when we were so near. Hiking felt good despite this radical change in temperature, a shift influenced not only through La Niña and cyclical changes in weather but also through the lifestyles we chose, our appetite for energy.

From behind a clump of Douglas fir, the snowboarder reappeared in a mist of kicked-up frost, his body curved atop the board to meet the road's bend. Ken and I stood frozen in place by his balance in the snow, a reminder of our own sleds flying down the cul-de-sac and the way we'd welcomed more moderate snowfalls growing up.

"Looks like fun," Ken said.

I nodded and said nothing, saving my breath for the mountain.

The summit came in a clearing of alder and an ice-coated radio tower humming in the wind, what Ken called the mountain singing. There wouldn't be a clear view of downtown Seattle, not with today's clouds and wind wrapping around the mountaintop. Twenty miles away, the city was still trapped in ice with residents immobilized by unplowed roads and the sand not working as planned.

Ken and I snapped a few photos of each other squinting into snow and wind.

"Let's go back," Ken said seconds later.

Gusting snow and gravity sent us downhill faster, our steps reaching for the tracks we'd already made in now-familiar snow. The wind lessened the further down we came, the skies still gray but less fierce than those at the summit.

At the house, ice from our hiking boots melted onto old newspapers placed by the heat vents. From the kitchen table, we watched tamer, lowland clouds bring an inch or two of fresh snow, which now seemed like nothing.

A few days after our hike, a warmer weather system replaced the winter storm. Forecasters feared that this change, like a drought ended by torrential rain, would flood local rivers and lakes with a deluge of melted snow. Numb to the reports by now, John and I took advantage of improved roads to drive along the coastline and visit my aunt two hours away. With the same deliberate optimism of the snowboarder we'd met, John guided the Trooper between the coastline's red-barked madrones, their branches grasping at the car like hands.

Although the region's streets were close to passable by now, the snowstorm's influence continued. Through its use of sand, the City of Seattle now had tons of the gritty substance to clean up to ensure bicycle and motorcycle rider safety. In the months to come, collected sand would clog a wastewater treatment plant, prompting a quick cleanup to avoid spills. The city adapted with a shift in its strategy. Amending a decade-old policy, Mayor Greg Nickels announced the city would salt its roads only during periods of extreme cold and more than four inches of snow.

Two winters later, another severe Northwest winter would be predicted, bringing a rare Thanksgiving snow and several wetter and a cooler than average summers. Central Texas, meanwhile, became embroiled in an exceptional drought, bringing a record-breaking string of 100-degree days.

"You found an opening in the storm," Aunt Delores said once we arrived at her home in Shelton and took her out for a late lunch at a favorite café, the three of us ducking from one dripping awning to the next. John and I relaxed, this particular system mild-mannered compared to the snowstorm we'd learned to live with.

The wind eased by the time we drove up Interstate 5 a few hours later, the tree branches wavering instead of reaching. Despite the calm of our drive past Olympia and Tacoma, the storms of our own making followed close. Remnants of this latest weather system nudged the Trooper along the freeway in quiet yet familiar gusts, no longer a stranger.

13

Earthquake Chaser

At Sea-Tac Airport, January darkness hid the mountain where I grew up. Normally, the Seattle area was my final travel destination, but this afternoon the airport was my second of three on the way to Fairbanks, Alaska, for a job interview. On their own adventures, high school students in letter jackets, teammates of a sport I couldn't identify, snapped gum and lolled in the vinyl chairs surrounding our gate. I still had several hours of waiting and flying to go before my day, which had started that morning in Austin, Texas, was complete. This trip reminded me of Aunt Delores and the seven years she'd lived in Alaska, a state mythologized for wilderness, resources, and geologic might.

When I told my aunt I was heading to Alaska for an interview, her face had lit up like the Northern Lights I hoped to see, even on a trip for business. In Shelton for a Christmas visit, I sat close to her black, square stove, a natural gas-powered version without smoke emissions.

Her mother, Sarah, had heated the house with a wood stove, its rounded sides warming the kitchen with the kindling it burned. Years later, my dad expanded Mom's kitchen with a wood-burning stove, although recent concerns about Puget Sound air quality and Dad's tolerance for cold meant it didn't get used as much, though I sometimes fired it up on my visits there.

At my aunt's house, the stove's quiet ticking proved an efficient substitute for crackling wood. I listened to Delores tell stories about Anchorage, Alaska, where she worked and married, leaving only when the earth trembled beneath her feet.

First settled by Alaska's Native peoples, including the Aleuts, Athabascans, Eskimos, Tlingit, and Haida, Europeans were later lured by the promises of fur, gold, copper, and eventually, oil. Even today, the non-Native population of Alaska is largely transient. After WWII, with Alaska approaching statehood, a new wave of explorers ventured into an area torn between development of abundant resources and preservation of wilderness areas such as Denali National Park and Preserve.

Delores ventured to Alaska in 1957, two years before it became a state. Similar to my own move to Austin, Delores moved to Anchorage with her friend Kay. While Kay worked for the FAA as a draftsman, Delores initially worked as a secretary for Cordova, a small airline at the Anchorage International Airport that flew into small mining/fishing villages. Delores told me her boss was a famous ex-Bush pilot, Merle K. Smith. Kay and Delores lived on adventure as much as their work, sometimes selecting a road to see where they'd end up and reconstructing home from unchartered territory.

During one of these road trips, their route grew more and more remote, until the pair lost track of where they'd been and considered abandoning the trip altogether.

"A little bit farther," Kay said.

Delores wasn't so sure. The waiting restaurant surprised them both. In a clearing, out of nowhere, appeared a building surrounded by parked cars. Unsure what this place was or whom it belonged to, Delores and Kay stepped carefully out of their car. Inside the door, they saw tables covered with linens and patrons dressed up for fine dining.

That's when Delores saw her boss sitting at a table. By that time, she'd started to embrace the adventure she and her friend had stumbled into, this landscape with ample surprises. "He asked us to join him at his table. So we did."

In swirling snow, my Alaska host drove her SUV on a two-lane road to Chena Hot Springs, a little over an hour outside of Fairbanks. I'd stepped into Alaska the night before wearing a borrowed puffy down coat. The snow was dry and light, squeaking beneath my hiking boots and powdered white as far as the eye could see.

My host pulled over a few miles outside of Fairbanks to show me the oil pipeline. Part of an eight-hundred-mile route from Prudhoe Bay to Valdez, the round pipe stood elevated by supports in this and other sections to minimize its impact on the permafrost. Completed in 1977 after a lengthy battle between oil companies and environmentalists, the Trans-Alaska Pipeline System, more than thirty years later, operates at a third of its peak production in 1988. Lower oil volumes cause lower oil temperatures throughout the pipeline, increasing the risk of its corrosion. Considering these declining production and safety issues, along with the high cost of oil, the state sought additional, renewable energy sources. Though my host took a picture of me standing next to the pipeline, the image was lost, dusk taking back the landscape.

With the snowfall thickening, we climbed back into the SUV, mist wrapping the car like fine gauze. A few other vehicles passed us, but for the most part, the road stayed clear. "If we see a car pulled over," my host explained, "it'd be illegal to not to stop and help."

The snow fell faster, hiding the road in front of us. From this trip alone, with limited road signs and fewer cars, it was easy to see the significance of this law, the difference it could make between survival and freezing to death.

"Does this road lead anywhere else?" I asked.

My host shook her head, her eyes straight ahead. "Just to the hot springs. Some of the employees live there."

The road ended, just as she'd said, at the hot springs resort with an overhead sign and the first lights I'd seen in miles. The snowfall had lightened by then, a star or two appearing over the parking lot. Greenhouses and outbuildings were scattered throughout the property. After plugging in the car so the battery wouldn't freeze, we headed to the main building and changing room, the overhead lights warming us despite the cold. Even the Northern Lights seemed possible given the patches of open sky.

We changed into swimsuits and water shoes, left our clothes in lockers, and carried our towels to warm water pools. Chena Hot Springs began from two faults intersecting deep beneath the surface, giving water warmed through travels in the earth's crust a pathway to the surface. My host eased us into an indoor pool first, its waters tepid rather than hot. Two businessmen talked shop nearby. After acclimating to the first pool, we stepped outside in our wet suits, stunning our bodies on a frost-lined pathway before sinking into the steam of an outdoor pool lined with black rocks and pockets of stars.

Poolside lights softened piles of snow lining the pool, its waters sulfur-scented. My host and I sat on a few of the submerged rocks, their sides smooth and algae-free. Mist from the warm waters froze our hair gray, an instant aging process. "Don't break the ice on your head," my host cautioned, "or you may take off some hair, too."

I nestled in the rocks, the water warming not only my body but also heating the entire resort. With its use of geothermal energy, an abundant Alaskan resource, Chena Hot Springs fueled its facility at a substantial cost savings compared to the use of diesel fuel.

The sulfur scent faded the longer we stayed, starlight now poking through the clouds and the water layering our hair in frost. Only a few other guests lingered nearby. With the early darkness making it feel later than it was, we grabbed our towels and hurried back to dry clothes and dinner at the resort. I considered trying on my aunt's adventure, her own reinvention.

Aunt Delores came home from work in Anchorage on Good Friday, March 27, 1964, and didn't feel like cooking. She picked up the phone to call Red and ask him to pick up hamburgers on his way home, a call she never finished. *The house started to shake,* she writes in her account of this day.

Having endured many earthquakes, I knew what was happening, waited for it to stop, and when it didn't, I grabbed our little Boston terrier, Penny (who was running around in circles in panic) and dived under the kitchen table.

And there we huddled while it happened. I remember a lot of noise (I had never heard anything like that before), groaning, grinding sounds, sounds of the house trying to keep its balance, sounds from the garage, where things were falling and it seemed to go on forever (it was actually a little under two minutes). I think that's what it will be like when the world comes to an end, only it won't stop at two minutes.

Because the shaking had been so violent, it took a while for things to stop moving when the quake itself was spent. And then, after all the noise, there was dead silence. I let Penny go and crawled out from under the table. My memory is a little fuzzy on what I did next, but I remember feeling a draft and saw that the sliding glass door had slid open and that it was starting to snow.

The next morning, the second day of my interview, my stomach flip-flopped—though my suite was stocked with fruit and yogurt, oatmeal and cereal, I couldn't manage to eat. It wasn't like me to be this nervous, yet I wasn't sure I'd eaten anything that would cause this, either. Gathering my notebook and puffy jacket, I climbed downstairs to meet my host, who was waiting in her warmed-up car below and ready to pick up our morning coffee.

"Do you mind stopping at a pharmacy?" I asked, not revealing too much.

She took us to a grocery store where I purchased some chewable antacid; the idea of a remedy made me feel better. The morning's meetings went by quickly, and at lunchtime, still with no appetite, I walked across the snow to a café, thinking the cold air might do me some good and ordering soup and crackers, all the while wondering how on earth yesterday's pad thai lunch and salmon dinner could have caused such grief. The sky had clouded over by now, the possibility for Northern Lights slim.

Back at my suite, I watched the sun go down early, not a sudden darkness but a deepening shade, a version of the 4:30 p.m. darkness I'd grown up with in Washington. There was only an hour before I'd be picked up for a tour around the city—I changed into jeans, warm socks, and hiking boots while the light disappeared. No more snow fell, though the sky matched the off-white snow in its promise of more to come. The skies offered a faint breeze compared to the stormy conditions from our drive the night before.

Wind power also has a place among alternative energy sources in Alaska, whether through traditional wind turbines placed on the state's abundant coastline, or through a floating turbine taking advantage of higher winds hundreds of feet up. With designs and locations taking both bird and bat flight patterns into account, these structures perched on island chains and hillsides created by deeper, older forces, the shifting plates far beneath the surface.

The earthquake of 1964 was the largest North American earthquake ever reported, its measurements between 8.2 to 9.2 on the Richter scale and similar to or slightly stronger than the 2011 earthquake in Japan. The number of lives lost in the 1964 earthquake was 131, mainly from the resulting tsunami that swept over the coastal areas of Alaska.

Earthquakes are cruel, because the initial shock itself is bad enough, has already scared you witless, but then it continues to torment you for weeks, months on end with aftershocks. We were to have over 900 before it was over, at first every five minutes it seemed so there was no peace for me. For quite a while I wore my clothes to bed, wouldn't sleep under the covers because I needed to be ready to run, always my first response when the ground starts to move.

The house Delores and Red lived in was not heavily damaged in the earthquake, other than a few things falling off the walls. Their power was restored quickly compared to other areas suffering much more damage, such as the inlet where an entire bluff broke off, taking houses with it. Delores didn't go back to her job at the FAA for a while, going to work with Red, instead, although eventually her boss at the time, Mr. Young, arrived at the door and asked if she wanted to go back to work. Because the eight-story building with their offices had been damaged, her boss, with a miner's light strapped to his forehead, climbed eight flights of an unlighted stairway to retrieve supplies and files they'd need.

On his first trip, Mr. Young came back with my typewriter strapped to his back, along with a pair of walking shoes that he'd spotted in my desk drawer—that made me cry, because in the midst of all that was going on, trying to keep our department running, he thought of me, that I might need those shoes. I was lucky that my typewriter was still sitting on my desk, just as I had left it because not everyone was so fortunate. When the building started swaying, picking up speed, loose objects, typewriters were thrown around, destroyed.

I've often wondered about the poor fellow who was on duty (on the eighth floor) the evening of the quake. He was up there all alone, with the building whipping back and forth, loose objects flying all around him. The story is that he had a breakdown, was never able to work again and I believe it.

Many of the people Delores and Red knew, coworkers and friends who'd come to Alaska for adventure and opportunity, didn't stay after the earthquake. Though some normalcy returned, the aftershocks made the event hard to forget. Delores and Red left Anchorage in 1964 after Red received a job offer from Cummins Diesel in Cleveland, Ohio.

In Ohio, Delores thought she'd be safe, but more than ten years later, she experienced the familiar tremors of an earthquake. This one registered a 2 or 3 on the Richter scale, not close to the massive earthquake she'd lived through in Anchorage, but enough to rattle her nerves, remembering.

I left Alaska so early it felt like nighttime, the snow packed tight in a dry squeak I'd grown used to after spending several days here, the sky still too cloudy for Northern Lights. I heard the shuttle honk and hustled my bag downstairs and lurched into the van. With nausea still dogging me, I closed my eyes and leaned against my bag to avoid the bumps along the way. Every now and then I'd sneak a glance at the passing trees hidden in snow, the shapes of mountains in the distance.

At the airport, I bought Imodium tables along with a silver bracelet inlaid with the shape of a moose, a reminder of the one I'd seen lumbering across the road. From the plane, a mountain poked its top through the clouds in a layer of first light. Even in my short stay here, one plagued with a stomach virus, I saw the lure of this place for second chances, its unpredictable power.

During my return half-hour layover in Seattle, the sun came out, warming the bench I sat on and bathing the airport in winter light. Western Washington, like Alaska, perched along fault lines. In 2001, the Seattle area faced an earthquake of 6.8, its epicenter eleven miles northeast of Olympia. Its rumblings were significant enough to bring Dad out of the house, not to hide under a table like our teachers had taught us in school but to go outside so he could see the ground move.

"I called your aunt to see if she wanted me to come down," he told me later. "She told me to stay home, that things were okay."

It was a good thing Dad didn't drive south, as parts of the route were badly damaged, including a landslide at Highway 101 on the way to my aunt's place. Seattle's Alaskan Way Viaduct, an elevated stretch of freeway along the water, was also heavily damaged from what had been dubbed "the Nisqually earthquake."

"The earthquakes are following her," my dad said about Delores, although I thought it might be the other way around, her attraction toward places with a fierce, unconventional energy.

A boarding call for my flight sounded for the last leg on this particular trip. On sun-warmed vinyl seats, I contemplated skipping my flight and staying in the Northwest, a change that would've cost me time and energy. Although I wouldn't land the Fairbanks job, my experience there widened the view of where I'd head next, toward my own shifting fault lines.

14

Unseen on Orcas Island

John and I shared a driftwood log on a rocky beach, the northernmost tip of Orcas Island. In the distance, a green and white ferryboat carried riders to another island in this chain of scattered, secret worlds. Located off the northernmost coast of Washington, the San Juan Islands were an ancient mountain range now hidden by water and home to bird and sea life. I'd visited them before, yet it took the distance of moving away and returning to get to know the islands and their secrets even better.

It was early March, the air moist but warm for this time of year in the Pacific Northwest. I wore a light fleece jacket, enough to get by. We walked back to the bed and breakfast where I was staying for a writing residency and where John, tempted by a getaway and a chance to look for bass wood, was visiting for the weekend, seeking a glimpse of this place reachable only by boat or plane.

A helicopter thudded overhead. "Must be some kind of tour," I murmured to John. Its low flight path seemed out of place on the islands during the offseason and not the best time for whale watching. Neither was it the preferred transportation method for its diverse residents.

Orcas Island was first home to the Straits Salish people and especially the Lummi, who call themselves "People of the Sea." With a culture centered on salmon fishing, the Lummi continue to fish in customary places both on and off reservation lands. British and American explorers traveled to these island outposts in the 1850s. Farming and fishing served as their primary industries, although the proximity of the island shores to Canada and the United States also proved ideal for smugglers.

Hours later, over a dinner of clam chowder in the nearby town of Eastsound, a woman brought John and me the bill and leaned against an empty chair as if ready to stay awhile. We were her only customers at this late hour. "Someone spotted the Barefoot Bandit," she said. "A helicopter searched for him today."

The night before, a broken window in a hardware store activated an alarm. The morning helicopter we'd heard scouring the island forests wasn't a tour group, but police from several counties and State Patrol joining forces to comb Eastsound. In addition to the air search, police explored the area on foot with canine tracking.

I rested my chowder spoon beside its white bowl. Colton Harris-Moore, also known as the "Barefoot Bandit," was accused of unusual break-ins and even more bizarre escapes. Since 2008, the teenager had been on the run after walking away from a juvenile detention center in Renton. He was suspected of crimes in the San Juan Islands, including stealing and flying a plane from Anacortes to Orcas Island, a feat he'd supposedly accomplished reading Internet flight manuals.

The woman eyed the cash register near the restaurant entry. "Last year, we lost $10,000—all that was left were footprints." I knew the ones she was talking about—rare, cartoonish-looking footprints had become the suspect's namesake and calling card.

After our meal, I had mixed feelings leaving the woman on her own in the narrow kitchen galley, though she waved us off with a cheerful good-bye, as if glad she had a chance to go home, too. Outside, the wet streets of Eastsound took on a different cast, opaque and hushed as the starless sky.

The next day, with John on a small plane bound for the mainland, I drove the Trooper to Moran Park for a hike. Many of the cabins I passed were boarded up, waiting for tourists or part-time residents saving their vacation days for summer. The largest of the San Juan Islands but not the most populated, Orcas Island offered plenty of opportunities to disappear.

At the trailhead, I parked the Trooper on a wide, visible shoulder. Rather than leave my small purse, an easy target through the Trooper's oversized windows, I stuffed it under my rain jacket. The bulge at my side looked obvious—I should've left it at the bed and breakfast, but it was better than not hiking at all. I rechecked the Trooper's locked doors, hoping no one would decide to borrow the aging vehicle and feeling alone outside of it, but not enough to avoid the hike altogether.

Sunshine faded the farther I walked into the old-growth forest of thickened trees both standing and on their sides, fallen logs forming lairs large enough to escape in. The forest stayed quiet, normal for this time of year, migratory birds wintering in other locations. Some birds, like the red-crested Pileated woodpecker I'd seen through the kitchen window of our bed and breakfast, were content to stay. The woodpecker hammered a trunk within easy sight of the house, its form silhouetted as if no one could see it.

I listened for larger signs of life, a throwback to the days when I'd run full tilt from Bigfoot. All I heard so far on the trail was a distant waterfall. I walked with purpose, not stopping to check the map, noting the scenery in quick glimpses rather than lingering over the rock piles left by other hikers.

Near the top of the trail, brush crackled. I almost looked around for our old dog Buffy, Mom beside her. But instead of the crashing I remembered, the steps I heard now stayed slow, deliberate. Around a hairpin turn a solo hiker appeared, her eyes not meeting mine. The medium-height woman stayed absorbed in her own pursuits, her steps following the same no-nonsense cadence as my own.

Once I reached the waterfall, I spent extra time around the stream, its chatter and driftwood familiar. On a bridge similar to the one Dad built across our own backyard creek, I crossed the stream, footsteps echoing across the timbers.

On the way back down the trail, my steps slowed enough to add rocks to trailside piles and admire the tallest Douglas fir. The trailhead spit me back into the light, making me blink after spending so much time in tangled growth. I held my breath walking across the road to reach the Trooper. Though I half-expected the boxy red rig to be gone, part of someone else's covert getaway, it was just where I'd left it, awaiting my own escape.

After a morning of writing, I drove the Trooper toward a ferry bound for neighboring San Juan Island and killer whales. Although it was the off season for the whales, which would be wintering further south this time of year, I could still visit the Whale Museum and explore the town. The Trooper passed blended woods, green fields, and gardens, morning clouds giving way to sun breaks. Parking the car in a spot above the ferry terminal, I wandered downhill on foot and waited with eight or so other foot passengers headed for Friday Harbor via free inter-island travel.

Onboard, I climbed to the upstairs observation deck, grabbed a French vanilla coffee from the vending machine, and sat down in one of the booth-style seats lining the windows to find a jigsaw puzzle in progress spread on the table, waiting for someone to solve it. Previous travelers had completed almost all of the shoreline and grass in the puzzle picture before leaving me with the sky, scattered pieces all the same shade of blue.

Past the boat's quick departure, the Orcas Island terminal and the island grew smaller. I fiddled with the scene in front of me, turning pieces in different ways to find a fit. Though I found a few snippets of blue sky on the floor, I imagined others forgotten down the vinyl seat or hidden in someone's pocket, a riddle no one would ever fully complete.

Several years ago, someone snuck into Dad's open garage in the middle of the day. This visitor had peered inside the silver sedan and left the car door wide open after hearing Dad inside the house. Whoever snuck into the rural setting must've come from the woods and escaped back into them on foot, was all Dad would say, some kid. There was no one running down the long driveway within view of the house, no vehicle spitting gravel in its wake. John wondered if it might've been a fugitive like the Barefoot Bandit, who was rumored to stay in numerous homes uninvited. In Dad's case, it never happened again.

The incomplete puzzle hastened my forty-minute ride, the green form of San Juan Island now in view. I finished my coffee and descended with the other foot passengers onto the footbridge between boat and the shore. Uphill, I followed my map into the town of Friday Harbor and found the museum site a street away.

The Whale Museum expanded from its small doorway to rooms of killer whales, gray whales, sea lions, and other sea life. One of the only guests during this midweek visit, I took my time learning about the Southern Resident killer whales living in the waters between northern Washington and southern British Columbia where the Strait of Juan de Fuca and the Strait of Georgia intersect. The whales based their interactions on family, traveling in J, K, and L pods.

I wove between the exhibits and overhead whale skeletons. Video showed Southern Residents viewed from the island's shore, black and white forms bursting from the water and reminding me what one of the other writers in the residency I was staying at had told me about watching them from her house, how she didn't need to venture farther than the shore.

I remembered the gray whale Dad pointed out, visible from the Ocean Shores jetty. The pods, too, had an option to keep us at a distance. Washington State and the federal government outlawed orca captures in the mid-1970s following the netting and seizing of more than forty orcas for aquariums. With the whale population facing slow growth after a low count of 80 in 2001, the Southern Resident population joined the federal Endangered Species list in 2005. Although protected from capture, a declining salmon population, water-quality issues, oil spills, and vessel proximity all posed threats to the whales' well-being.

After a few hours in the museum, I left with a new fleece-lined rain jacket from the gift shop and directions to a café up the street. From a seat overlooking the harbor, I ate clam chowder and a sandwich. Seagulls, savvy year-round residents, skimmed the waters for windfalls. On a late afternoon trip back to Orcas Island, I stood on the deck watching the ferry glide through green waves, a covert home just beneath the surface.

John and I flew up to the Northwest a year after the writing residency and caught a ferry to Orcas Island during one of the sunniest days of a cool summer. We'd planned a ferry ride to neighboring San Juan Island's Lime Kiln Point State Park in search of whales, along with an Orcas Island visit to a wood dealer, someone who milled fallen trees for musical instruments.

John's older brother, Karl, and Karl's partner, Leah, both living in Vancouver, Washington, joined us in Dad's Trooper from Issaquah to Anacortes. Karl and John, born a scant few years apart, shared similar height, hair, and voice, people often mistaking them for one another. Leah rolled down her window to let in the warmth after days of rain.

In the town of Eastsound, the skies were as blue as the puzzle I'd worked on during my last visit. Windsocks floated above the store awnings and most doors stood open wide, shop owners relaxed compared to our previous visit when worries of the Barefoot Bandit ran fresh.

Apprehended in the Bahamas following a boat chase, Colton Harris-Moore served a sentence for state crimes in Stafford Creek Corrections Center, Aberdeen. As part of a plea agreement in response to federal charges, proceeds from a movie deal estimated at more than a $1 million would go toward the restitution of stolen property, including planes.

Leah leaned her petite form against one of the flowerboxes. "It's a perfect day," she said, content no matter what our hours here offered.

"No cell service," John said. He stared at the phone, as if willing it to reveal the location of the wood dealer.

"I could find it," I said, relying on my visit the time before when I'd picked up a piece of wood for John. All four of us climbed into the Troop-

er and left Eastsound, curving around Crescent Beach and its shore layered in rocks and sand. Past inland forest and fields of horses, we drove
under the Moran Park arches to Cascade Lake, its water full of scattered
light. After driving through the community of Olga, I pointed up a steep
driveway. John kept the Trooper slow in case we ran into deer.

At the end of the wooded driveway, the yard was a little too quiet, the
wood mill's doors closed and no one in sight. John stepped out to knock
just in case. He walked back to the Trooper, his reappearance telling us
we'd missed our window to meet the wood dealer, although it gave us
an excuse to return to the island. We stopped for lunch at Café Olga, a
restaurant and gallery repurposed from a strawberry-barreling barn. We
took our time over blackberry pie, a fresh version of the tangled fruit I'd
grown up with.

Driving through Moran Park, we weighed our options. If we hurried,
we could reach San Juan Island by ferry and take a bus to the west side
of the island and possibly spot the Southern Resident killer whales, which
numbered 82 in 2013. A federal law adopted in 2011 made it illegal for
boats, including kayaks and sailboats, to come within two hundred yards
of the Southern Residents, a regulation designed to limit the increasing
water traffic following them.

"Or we could hike here," I said, trading a hectic pace for the skimming
approach of the seagulls. If Southern Resident killer whales roamed west
of San Juan Island on this sunny day, the idea of them persisting there was
good enough.

With Leah already near the trail, Karl and John followed a step behind
her on a path stretching up to Mount Constitution. John and I lingered
to feel the bark of cedar and Douglas Fir along the way. We heard rather
than saw birds in their quick trips from one covert place to another, keeping their hiding places to themselves. Passing old-growth trees so large we
couldn't put our arms around them, we smelled the weeks of rain in the
mix of standing and fallen trees.

"Are we close?" Leah asked a hiker in shorts and a hat, the only other
person we met on the trail during an hour-long ascent. Neither he nor his
companion breathed very hard.

"Halfway, or maybe a little more," the man said.

I considered the rest of the distance, whether it was a milestone that
mattered. Dad was expecting us for dinner, and it would take at least another hour to reach the 2,400-foot summit, not to mention our return. I
pictured the 1930s rock tower we'd driven to on our last trip. Built during

the Depression-era New Deal program, it offered a bird's eye view of sky, water, and islands.

"We could go back," Leah offered. Though she could've reached the summit with ease, she was just as flexible returning, the hike its own incentive.

The unreached panorama nagged me at first, though I was better off focusing on the steepest parts of the trail and looking forward instead of back. I admired the aged Douglas fir along the path instead, the way the ferns reached out in gray-green fingers. In one dim patch of overgrowth, I felt eyes staring. It was easy to ignore at first, hearing Ken's words from years ago, *probably a deer*. I searched for a doe or speckled fawns in this mix of conifers and deciduous trees.

It took a few seconds to see the owl on a branch about thirty feet away. White and brown-checkered body camouflaged against a tree, its cream-white face floated in the shadow, eyes wide as my own. "Look," I whispered to John.

The owl swiveled its head to take in all four of us in its home of old growth. We spent a few minutes blinking at each other before Leah and Karl took several quiet steps forward. Although the path took us closer to the owl's hold on an outstretched limb—I was certain it would fly away—the bird held its ground, a quiet, patterned sentinel, a reminder of the grove of owls we'd grown up with.

We made good time down the rest of the trail, endorphins and what I later decided was a barred owl making up for the bass wood and whales we missed that day. With our breathing back to normal, we breezed the Trooper through the park entrance and back to Eastsound, rolling down the car windows along the way to smell the grass and water. Past grazing goats, bed and breakfast signs, and a quick stop at Darvill's bookstore, we arrived at the terminal about a half hour early.

Before we spotted the water at the dock, we saw cars, rows of them stacked up to meet the ferry. John edged the Trooper in line with the rest of the traffic. I searched the harbor below, hopeful we'd make it and fiddling with the pages of a John McPhee book I'd just bought.

Our line of cars crawled to a stop. One of the employees stopped us several car lengths from the landing, an assurance we weren't making this trip and dinner at Dad's. I turned on my cell phone, which offered no service.

"We'll find a public phone," said Karl, who led me out of the car and into the ferry terminal office with a phone book and no phone in sight.

"There used to be a phone booth at the bottom of the hill," said a woman, as if I'd been referring to something vintage. Her words stayed slow, as if she were considering other small, imperceptible changes over time.

John and I plotted our next move. Although we might've gained better cell phone reception driving somewhere else, it meant losing our place in line and a bump to an even later ferry. In flashes of brown and white, cotton-tailed rabbits sped across the ferry dock lawns, already home but no less harried.

Karl ducked inside the 1904 Orcas Hotel and returned with a look of success. "We can use their phone," he said.

A woman in her twenties led us to a banquet room of the Victorian-style hotel with period furniture and a modern phone sitting on a side table. I dialed Dad's house, willing him to answer this unknown number on caller ID. "Hello," he said in his usual, back-East lilt. He was easy about the missed ferry, the steaks we'd chosen saved for another day. Instead, we planned a Sunday breakfast with sausage, pancakes, and eggs, a meal all of us would pitch in and cook at his house on the mountain.

With an hour-and-a-half wait ahead of us, followed by a ferry trip and car ride, a journey that would bring us to Dad's about midnight, Leah and I ordered clam chowder, fish and chips baskets, and hard cider from the hotel café. The afternoon turned a soft gold, the air cool with approaching fall. The four of us sat at a metal table near other customers who'd missed the ferry and traded expectations for a longer view, distant foothills waiting.

15

Light in the Trees

$\int$ quak Mountain, normally freckled with household lights on the way up, was black. I stared where Dad, who was driving the silver sedan, pointed, a slope that looked desolate compared to the crowded airport we'd just left. A year and a half after Karyl died, we made our Christmas trek from Texas to Dad's, a home perched between the constant of forested hills and the growth of nearby cities. From the back seat—I left the front seat to Dad and John, both of them long-legged—I watched our mountain, a foothill to the Cascades, grow larger and darker than the night sky surrounding it.

"Still no power," Dad said. His words were matter-of-fact.

In a home hidden by trees, with lights no one could see from the dead-end road below it, my family was used to being without electricity for a few hours. When fallen branches toppled power lines or an ice storm snapped cables, we were ready. Dad would dig out the flashlights with fresh batteries. Ken would pull a camping lantern out of the hall closet. Mom stuffed another log in the wood stove, and we all waited for light to fill the room, too bright from the switches we'd forgotten didn't work and flipped on while we stumbled around the house.

This time, deep in a mid-December night, a windstorm proved angrier and the Seattle area more populated, an uneasy combination resulting in fifteen deaths and more than a million homes and businesses without power. In the wake of sixty-nine mile an hour winds coursing across western Washington, both local and out-of-state crews made repairs that couldn't be rushed. A neighborhood at a time, they restored the electricity, heat, and hot water most of us took for granted.

By the time John and I arrived from Texas, Dad had been without power for four days. Issaquah was still slowly coming back to life following business and school closures; some still scrambled for necessities such as food and fuel. Adding to the difficulties in the days following the storm, temperatures plunged into the twenties at night.

I'd been relieved to see Dad at the airport—he was unreachable by phone since the storm hit. Still, I knew he had a generator, two wood stoves, a portable radio, and resilience that made him look and act fifteen years younger than his actual age of eighty. It wasn't a big surprise to see him at the airport as we'd arranged a few weeks before, near our usual meeting place by the baggage carousels.

"You can use my cell phone," I told him.

He was glad I brought it, but not for himself. "That's good, he said. "You can call your aunt."

His strength made me look harder at myself, softened by access to everything and unprepared for disaster. I'd spent more years growing up on the mountain than apart from it, yet still worried I'd forgotten how to live in this revised version of home. I didn't know how I'd handle losing power for a few days, or if I could manage gracefully without it. Even generators needed fuel to run them, and without electricity, most of the area's gas pumps weren't functioning. Dad, who was ready with a few spare gallons when the storm hit, found a remote service station to refuel the generator a couple of days later. Five cars soon lined up behind him.

The tank of the sedan was still close to full. The closer we drove to home, the thicker the blackness, with neither fluorescent streetlights nor blinking Christmas strings. Instead, a few tiny squares of household light, powered by candlelight or generators, shone from single rooms. Our driveway carved a tunnel between the trees. It was almost as dark as the days before anyone lived there but bear, deer, and coyote, whose visits had grown more frequent.

Once outside the car, instead of the rumbling creek, we heard the hum of a generator from a distant house. Inside, the coals from the wood stove burned red. It was enough to illuminate our faces when we gathered at the kitchen table to hear about the two hemlocks Dad lost in the storm. November's rain, a record fifteen inches, might have contributed to the fallen trees—it was hard to tell if the wet earth, wind, disease, or a combination of all three weakened them most. This winter, area residents and the forest shared a more troubled relationship than usual, violent weather mixing the two and having the last laugh.

I added another log to the fire and listened to the cedar pop. We divided the flashlights and toted our travel bags into the bedroom, Dad firing up the generator so we'd have enough light to put away our things and brush our teeth. We piled on the blankets and wore our thickest pajamas, enough to last until morning when the stove's warmth faded and the lights might just flicker back.

John and I woke to the rain and a crackling portable radio, along with Dad pawing through a dark refrigerator without complaint. "The milk should be all right," he said. "I run the generator just enough to power it, along with the microwave."

"What have you been eating?" I asked.

He made a face. "Cans of stuff I'll never eat again," he said. "Chili, beans. All pretty bad."

On the kitchen counter, Dad piled condiments and leftovers he suspected hadn't made it from the days of tepid cool. The half-used ketchup and mustard bottles probably also contained foods he simply didn't like or was sick of, which I supported given his bout with food poisoning a few years ago. After that, whenever he asked me about even the most recent leftovers from generous meals, I told him to toss them, preferring to waste food rather than risk it; neither Mom nor Karyl were around to help throw things out anymore.

We poured the milk over our cereal and hoped for the best. I thought of our own house near downtown Austin, the one we'd returned to after school, whether we had enough food to get by if a tornado or flash flood hit. I saw our frozen meats spoiling in the balmy winter, vegetables rotting, sugary snacks that would only make us hungrier, bottled water we didn't have at all. Never mind living off the land—I wouldn't do well living off our foods on hand. The morning paper talked about people not sharing their names because they were embarrassed at being caught off guard. Many of them escaped to hotels, friends who lived outside the area, or local stores.

I scanned the dingy bottles sitting on Dad's counter and the gray clouds outside. As a teenager, I turned to the city for adventure and escape. "Christmas shopping will get us out of the house for a while," I said.

John poured Rice Krispies in his bowl and shook his head at me in a teasing way, as if to say I'd use any excuse for shopping.

Dad nodded. "We'll eat a couple of meals out," he said.

"When do we pick up the turkey?" I asked.

Dad looked at his careful notes on the calendar. "Saturday," he said.

It was Wednesday, and Christmas Eve was on Sunday. The power might be on by then, maybe. Between crackles, the radio kept a persistent buzz about neighborhoods still without power. Earlier reports shared stories of freezing residents swapping food for firewood, or a space heater for some gas to power a generator. Area shelters and hotels were full. "If my phone had worked, I could have offered something, too," Dad said. We shut off the radio in the middle of its latest list of updates, people still in the dark.

Outside, cold rain fell. John piloted the sedan carefully down the driveway while I sat beside him and Dad lounged in the back. The further we drove from the trees and the closer to Renton, the more lights we saw popping up along the way. Everyone else must have had the same idea about getting out of the house and into the city, because the wet roads leading to the mall were crowded with cars. Inside the sedans, their faces were just like ours, blurred and bundled.

Once inside the bright aisles, a stark contrast to the darkness at home, we found a stand for Frango chocolates. Dad picked up a box wrapped in green and silver paper and handed it to the cashier along with his Nordstrom credit card.

The woman, who looked about twenty, swiped the card a few times before setting it down. "I'm sorry, but it isn't working," she said. She turned the card around to see if the other side worked.

Dad frowned. "They just sent me a new one," he said.

I glanced at the line behind us. Frango chocolates, first sold by Frederick & Nelson's, were later picked up by The Bon Marche and now belonged to Macy's, a parade of stores over the years that didn't include Nordstrom. It was a Christmas tradition for us, an urban update I'd kept track of. "A Nordstrom card won't work, Dad. I have a Macy's if you want."

"Oh, you're right," Dad said with a laugh. Even the cashier grinned. The line fanned out behind us, complete with a man dressed for work who looked annoyed with our exchange. My dad, I wanted to tell this impatient stranger, was a survivor in more important ways, someone who hadn't forgotten how to live in the trees.

Later, over an early dinner, John looked up from his baked potato. "Maybe the power will be on when we get back to the house," he said.

I passed the bread around and gave him a doubtful smile. The areas east of Seattle, where Dad lived, were hardest hit. All day, we'd heard stories of just-restored power, along with those still without it, including our waiter. "I bet it's off," I said.

Dad nodded his head in agreement. "I'm with Gail."

John laughed at us. "Not very optimistic," he teased.

I shrugged and refocused on my steak. I was getting used to life in the dark again, both from memory and from the perspective time lent. We weren't suffering, considering the occasional heat from the generator, the warmth of the wood stove, and the candy bars Dad kept in the snack drawer, not to mention easy access to escapes like shopping and eating out. The storms of my past came back with greater clarity. Ten years ago, a coating of ice shut down the Northwest and snapped its power lines. For a few days, I fired up the upstairs wood stove and Dad ran the generator, then brand new. It was the first Christmas after Mom died without warning, the storm an easier bleakness to navigate.

The evening rain on our way home made it look more like 10 p.m. than the time it really was, 7 p.m. We drove through the Renton Highlands, past the Greenwood Cemetery where Jimi Hendrix rested. Although we'd later visit the site, on this trip, John kept going, not even stopping for the lit grocery stores along the way.

The lower gear of the car told me we'd reached the mountain. Dad, John, and I tried to decide if the squares of light along the way were made by candlelight, generators, or just returned power.

In the driveway, John answered his own question by squeezing the garage door opener. The door didn't budge. "Guess you two were right," he said.

While John and I carried the bags inside, Dad stayed in the garage to turn on the generator for the fridge and a few lights. In the dim light, I imagined the crashing sounds Dad heard when the trees fell, though the impact to his house was distant; others weren't so lucky. The storm took fifteen lives, some from fallen trees and power lines, eight from carbon-monoxide poisoning.

I called my brother, who was also without power. "Dad hasn't had power for the last five days, and he lost two trees, but everything's fine," I said.

Ken's pause on the other end of the line told me he'd need to come see for himself. After I hung up the phone, I turned to Dad. "Ken's coming tomorrow for a hike," I said. "He wants to see the two trees that fell." I didn't mention he probably wanted to check on us, too.

Dad looked up from the weather report he was listening to and smiled as though he knew. "Tomorrow's your best day, weather-wise," he said. "Maybe we'll even have power."

* * *

The next morning, Dad flipped a switch and a soft glow answered. We could dry our hair without the help of a generator or go to the grocery store without fearing our food would spoil. Having power after living a few days without it was a luxury. I couldn't imagine what six days must have felt like to Dad, not to mention the extra days, as many as ten, those residents in outlying areas still faced.

The radio station, after a brief mention of the last areas without power, held a contest for listeners to name the storm, the eventual winner "the Hanukkah Eve Storm." In the coming weeks, the blast of wind would become one of last year's memories. It'd be easy to slip back into a comfort zone, too busy for natural calamities larger and stronger than the best-planned development.

My brother arrived at the house carrying a jacket for the rain and waffle-treaded boots. Instead of staying inside and enjoying the newfound warmth, we decided to go hiking and meet the forest on its own terms. Dad, who'd seen the trees, chose to stay home and lent John his hiking boots. I looked for one of Mom's coats in the closet, the outdoor ones she'd use for weeding the garden or walking in the woods, but they were long gone. I took one of Dad's smallest jackets instead.

Once we'd found enough clothes to keep us warm, John and I followed Ken down the trail behind the house. We soon reached the creek where the two trees fell. They were bigger than I'd imagined, a two-foot diameter trunk resting along the ravine and another just as large splayed across the creek. Sodden ground near the roots made it look as if they'd slid.

"How old do you think they are?" John asked.

Ken peered at their rough-barked sides. "Around eighty years, maybe a hundred."

All three of us stared at the heft of those almost invulnerable hemlocks, each representing a life that more than doubled ours. We walked across the bridge Dad built years ago and climbed the ravine on the other side of the creek. The ground felt more rain-soaked and soggy than I remembered, my black suede sneakers sinking in the mud. We chose the gravel road for easier walking, following its zig-zag path up the mountain. This combined state and county land of 2,500 acres was for now left to itself. And while at first glance it looked the same as years past, it'd been quietly shifting all along.

Forty minutes later, sunshine slipped between the trees and fell across our faces. In the thin warmth, I took off my jacket and forgot the power we'd rediscovered at home.

Ken slowed his pace so we could keep up. "We're almost there," he said. His long legs took the mountain's hairpin turns in easy strides.

Although my own legs protested during the first part of our hike, they found new energy at the summit. I glanced at the microwave tower perched at the top and followed Ken and John to a clearing near the edge of the ridge. Snow lay in patches at our feet. Without its summer foliage, the barren crest in front of us opened up a distant view of downtown Seattle.

I followed my brother's line of sight down the mountain and into the lowlands. Stray clouds muted the sunlight. From the edge of the summit, we stared seventeen miles away at a cluster of miniature skyscrapers.

"See the Space Needle?" my brother said.

I squinted through my contact lenses and made out the Needle's thin stem and round top. Towns in between, from Issaquah to Bellevue to Mercer Island and the floating bridge, stayed hidden in the mountain's shadow. From a few thousand feet up, evergreens started below our feet and ran downhill until they lapped up against the skyscrapers. It looked as if the forest was sharing space with the city rather than the other way around.

"Do you want to go down by the road again, or the trails?" my brother asked.

John moved his glance from the tiny buildings below us to the path my brother pointed to. "Let's take the trail," he said.

Ken led us to the trailhead and nodded at a few of the wooden signs we passed. "From one of these trails, you can walk to downtown Issaquah." His stride lengthened. "We're not too far from Mom's grave."

I looked in the direction where the graveyard must be, partway down the mountain and close to town. It was a good resting place. This foothill between the city and the mountains was the home she chose in the trees, the same complicated terrain I kept returning to.

The trail started out in a steep descent. I looked around to see if other trees had fallen, but most of them, safe in numbers that created a natural windbreak, were untouched. We saw only an occasional fallen tree along the trail, like the one splayed across a wooden picnic table at the old campsite at the summit, once a summer home owned by the Bullitt family. I stared at the table, the only evidence of civilization in sight, which was nearly split in two.

Halfway down, the trail sloped more gently. Mist slipped through the hemlocks, moss hanging from their branches like shawls. Beads of rain on evergreen needles turned to wet diamonds in the sun. Even in street shoes, walking in the woods came easier now. I showed John the smooth-leaved Salal and the spikier Oregon grape. We touched a cedar's sides, which ran in thin strips instead of chunkier Douglas fir bark. The trail wasn't so steep, its switchbacks, a compromise reached with the mountain, more manageable. We wove between the trees, finding our way back home.

16
Through the Smoke

Brown haze hid the mountains we drove toward, a shroud having nothing to do with rain. Replacing the usual soft blue horizon, smoke covered the top half of the Cascades, their peaks hazy and indistinct. The closer John and I drove east on I-90, about an hour from my hometown, the more this gritty curtain took hold, clouding our expectations. Hidden mountains were enough to make me reconsider our hike at Franklin Falls, just off I-90 near Snoqualmie Pass and site of old-growth forest, Douglas firs untouched by logging or the freeway.

We'd hiked there ten years ago near the summit of the pass, the lowest crossing in the Cascade Mountains and a route first used by Native Americans. Wagon trains later traversed this passage, the ruts of their wheels still visible in places near the Franklin Falls trail. The Sunset Highway, constructed in 1915, mirrored this east-west wagon route, a precursor of what would become Interstate 90 in the 1950s. A route still in transition, freeway updates east of the mountains included corridors for fish and wildlife, with culverts and bridges designed to help various species navigate changeable terrain.

The last time John and I hiked the short route to Franklin Falls, a waterfall at the south fork of the Snoqualmie River, it was a smoke-free, late-summer day. And while seasonal dryness was normal, the hike I remembered offered the sharp scent of Douglas fir along the river and a seventy-foot waterfall crashing into rocks and muting the sounds of trucks on the nearby overpass. This year, fire east of these mountains created the film we now drove into, part of a wildfire season burning longer, later, and with greater intensity than usual. Fire suppression combined with an unusually dry summer sustained a series of blazes in the state, among them the Taylor Bridge fire. This fire, determined by the Washington State Department of Natural Resources to have originated at a building site, burned more than twenty thousand acres and destroyed sixty homes in the mountains near Cle Elum, a town thirty miles east of Snoqualmie Pass.

My dad warned us about the dry weather before our annual summer visit to the area. It was the winter Northwest trips we usually remembered and named, like the year of the windstorm from a week-long power outage in December. This time, it was the summer journey we'd remember most, the year of smoke and fire and a sign the area was no more static than our own lives.

Close to Franklin Falls, the pungent grit was like driving into a campfire, intensifying my doubts. "The exit's closed," John said, blocked for construction rather than fire, orange cones fronting our turnoff. Dad's Trooper crawled by the exit and kept going up the pass, trucks to our right slowing at the steeper incline. Although we'd opened the windows to let in the breeze, we closed them just as fast to block the smoke. The ski resort summit we turned around at was bare and brown, an empty chair lift heading into the haze.

We looped back west onto the freeway to join semis barreling downward, the air still smoke-tinged even though we were driving away from fire. The westbound exit to the trails, unlike the eastbound exit, was open, prompting a quick turnoff and a search for the falls, their unlikely location in the Denny Creek area split between eastbound and westbound I-90.

"I remember this," John said, finding his way back to the scenery we'd visited years before, the sky white-washed but the forest still thick. Mature fir trees interspersed with fallen logs and younger trees, a diverse, aging forest yet still susceptible to the threat of fire.

During the summer of 2012, National climatic data from September reported many Northwest cities facing their driest periods ever. Although not topping a record of fifty-one days without rain set in 1951, the year had come close with forty-eight days, a stretch broken by a few hundredths of an inch of rain. It was enough to count for the record books but not enough to break the dry spell, the creek behind my dad's house reduced to a cool murmur, shifting weather patterns playing their own role in the expanding reach of fire.

We reached the Denny Creek campsite and a few empty tents, their occupants out hiking. A sign told us we'd need a day pass available from the summit we'd just left. I considered the dulled landscape outside the car, the still air, and the smoke. Today's midweek quiet would've been perfect for a walk in the woods, but the poor air quality didn't make backtracking up to the pass seem worth it.

"We could go to Snoqualmie Falls," I said. Made famous from the 1990s TV drama *Twin Peaks*, the Snoqualmie River combined its south, north, and middle forks, three alpine rivers culminating in a 268-foot plummet. At the first breath of my suggestion, John turned the car around and back onto the feeder road toward the freeway, Franklin Falls saved for another trip.

Westbound on I-90, the smoke scent transitioned to the smell of brakes from a truck slowing on this steep grade. The further west we drove, the greater the evidence of this burgeoning area, from new homes to apartments to stores. Despite signs of rapid expansion, parking at the site was easy on a Monday, a view of the falls just a footbridge away.

From a viewpoint just past the Salish Lodge, we watched water tumble in plumes thinned due to the dry weather this season. During a snowmelt, I remembered the waterfall widening over the sheer rock face, its thunderous voice silencing those on the viewing platform. Years ago, I'd taken a winter picture of my parents at the falls, capturing them in frozen mist.

Once we'd spent a few minutes tracing the water's slow-motion route from top to bottom, I searched for a trail easing down toward the base of the falls, a viewpoint with a different perspective. The Snoqualmie Tribe, or People of the Moon, had settled the region below the falls in addition to the river's upper plain, regions rich in salmon and game, respectively. The falls, listed on the National Register of Historic Places, have remained a site of natural, cultural, and spiritual confluence.

I felt turned around in this familiar place, every pathway I took ending up in fresh dirt and orange construction fencing, the trail inaccessible. Signage revealed Puget Sound Energy was both renovating the trail and making improvements to its one-hundred-year-old hydroelectric plant, the falls a complex site and home of more than one form of power. At the Snoqualmie Falls gift shop, I bought a box of pancake mix and asked the woman behind the counter about the fenced-off portion of trail. "It's closed for renovations until March of next year," she said. "Once it's done, it'll be really nice." Area growth had created not only a need for energy but also amenities like trails and necessities like fire protection. Of particular concern were residences located within the intersections of urban and rural, the same type of area I'd grown up in.

Driving up I-5 after a weekend in Portland with Karl and Leah, I searched for smoke I'd seen hovering near Mount Hood. East of the mountains, a fire along Highway 141 had threatened 500 houses in a rural area before firefighters could contain it, smoke we couldn't see from our current vantage point. Green road signs flitted against a blue-skied background, one of them for Ryderwood, the logging camp-turned retirement community my grandparents had lived in years ago. John, noticing my eyes on the sign, slowed the car. "Do you want to stop?"

I considered traveling down a road I hadn't been on in thirty years, a drive I remembered as forty miles or longer. "If it's too far, let's skip it."

John took the exit and stopped at a "T" in the road. A road sign displayed the mileage to Ryderwood. "Nine miles," John said, in case I'd missed it.

I stared at the single digit, a route I remembered as four times the distance. We passed a gas station and a café in place of the stand we'd stopped at for burgers and milkshakes years ago, comfort food to take us the rest of the way to our grandparents' house. We'd eaten at a picnic table or in the car, the details fuzzy, only the burnt goodness remaining. After lunch, the drive to Ryderwood had felt more like a carnival ride than a road, the station wagon's momentum sliding me from one side of the backseat to another. A few times, I arrived at Grandma's sick to my stomach.

"It's all these turns," John said, clarifying both the distance and my nausea. Even from today's front seat view, the road took its time and veered between farms, some lined in trim-painted fences, others piled with rusting equipment. Past Vader, population 600, the houses grew sparse and scattered. A series of Burma shave signs edged the highway, just as they had three decades ago, each one spaced wide apart for roadside reading. "It's about a Christmas tree farm closing," I said. It was an ending we happened to witness, signs I stared at long after the final message with its concluding rhyme.

The last few miles, forested hills grew up around the small town we couldn't see quite yet, the sky offering none of the smoke that had characterized this trip so far. The Long-Bell Company, which established a logging camp here, was among the first companies in the area to practice reforestation. An account from the University of Washington Forestry Department describes a tree nursery established in Ryderwood in 1926 with 13,000 acres of Douglas fir, cedar, and redwood. Area fires took their toll on the project, and after the start of the depression in 1931, the company halted the program. Of the original acreage planting, only 5,400 acres of the new plantings survived. With Long-Bell selling the area as a retirement community in the 1950s, second-growth trees remained to soften the hillsides.

The old logging camp turned retirement community appeared from between hillsides just like it always had in compact rows of 1920s bungalows. "There's the store," I said, closed for the day so we couldn't step inside, but still with a porch and a bench out front. I could almost see the man from years before, complaining about me following my brother.

Past the store, I realized I didn't have the address of my grandparent's old house, a location I'd known by feel rather than by number. "It was on a corner, maybe one house in." We drove up and down the rows of houses, their reds and custards and moss greens, all smaller than I remembered. The sun lounged the last half hour or so before twilight, the surrounding hillsides lighter than the valley below. This lowland location enclosed by woods had prompted citizens to clear brush and pick up piles of timber, a partnership with nonprofit Firewise helping prevent the spread of fire through the tight rows of houses.

With the Trooper at a crawl, I searched for the pink-gray siding of the house and its pointed white fence, the gravel alley Ken and I raced down on the three-wheeled bike. It was hard to know what it might look like now, its color and yard reimagined. John and I offered our own transformations, adaptability over time and from other places most of all.

Fronted with a "for sale" sign, one red house with a brown fence had the picture windows I remembered, the rattling plastic for storm windows replaced by something sturdier. Despite the cracked cement stairs, darker siding, and a missing porch, I recognized the gentle peaked roof, the maple trees I used to climb across the street.

"It's this one," I told John, who slowed and stopped. I imagined the wood stove in the kitchen, the corner cabinets where Grandma kept glass cats, the bathroom Dad spent hours updating. The front of the house was all we'd see, though I'd look it up later on a real estate website to view the kitchen interior with its arched doorway and the spare room floor I'd slept on, the flowerbeds and gnome in the backyard long gone.

I murmured the address, relegating it to memory. John turned around so we could drive by the house one more time, although I didn't want to leave the past just yet. "The lake's in the back of the neighborhood." I directed him toward what I thought was a street, but turned out to be an alley, one he had to back the Trooper out of.

"We need to go," John said. "People will think we're casing the joint."

I nodded, the dim light and hazy remembrances working against us, the aerial view I'd look up later showing a pond instead of a lake.

The Trooper breezed down the main street we'd come in on, the only way in and out of Ryderwood. A man standing in his yard just beyond the grocery store stopped and tracked the Trooper with his eyes, just like the man in front of the store years ago, his presence following us outside Ryderwood and its entrance sign, *Life is what you make it.*

The road spun us back into the countryside, curving toward the present. I turned around in my seat, facing forward again. "Did you see the guy looking at us?"

John's eyes stayed on the road, the turns coming up faster. "That place was a little scary."

I wondered whether it'd been a little weathered all along, my attention caught up in the speckled ducks I used to feed and the books I read in a living room patterned in rose-covered carpet. The area had changed in other ways, navigating not only wildfire risk but also its identity. A 2010 lawsuit debated the community's retirement status, some residents wanting Ryderwood open to a wider demographic. In a settlement four years later, a judge confirmed the area's retirement designation, prompting some residents to leave.

Back on the freeway, the distance from Ryderwood lengthened. Though its blackberry vines and logging paths still wove through my mind, the bungalow itself was something I'd moved on from. Revisiting its frame, only the look from a stranger was the same, a resident shooing us back to our own time.

On one of the last days of our Northwest trip, Ken and I walked through the perfume of Grandma's honeysuckle, a starter Mom brought from Ryderwood to Squak Mountain. Between Dad's backyard and Corinne's, we passed a field of bleeding heart, the purple and magenta flowers bent over in their shady hideout. Wandering up the mountain was both familiar territory and an answer to the hike escaping me so far on this trip—today's gray sky came not from smoke, but from cloud cover muting the Douglas fir, cedar, and hemlock along the road. We glided past the familiar trail through the woods to the more difficult part, the steep yet direct summit the old gravel road provided.

In addition to this straightforward, no-nonsense route, thirteen miles of hiking trails and six miles of horse trails now wove through the mountain parkland. In its most recent acquisition, King County, in conjunction with the Trust for Public Land, purchased 226 acres that had been slated for logging. Area citizens and groups such as the Issaquah Alps Trails

Club, concerned about runoff in May Creek and the impact to fish and wildlife, spurred an effort to preserve this latest portion of Squak Mountain, an area now set aside for recreation and wildlife habitat.

Rounding a hairpin turn, the trees thinned for a glimpse of Mount Rainier etched in lavender. I stopped both to look and to rest, breathing deeply enough to notice the air tinged with a hint of smoke. It wasn't as thick as the grit we'd experienced in Snoqualmie Pass from the fires in eastern Washington, but noticeable just the same. I couldn't tell if it was the smoke, the altitude, or my allergies, but I stopped several times to catch my breath.

Years ago, at a practice burn I wrote about for a weekly paper in Sumner, my breathing came just as fast. I'd planned to write the story from a distance, relying on notes rather than lived experience, until a firefighter handed me an oversized coat, hat, and boots. I followed the men in training through what was left of the house, water dripping from its charred sides, waves of smoke heading straight for us. We crawled on our elbows through the debris and blackened doorframes, just beneath the smoke. The air tasted sweet once we'd made our way out of what remained of somebody's home, no bigger than my grandparents' house, now just a shell.

I thought of Dad during each year's dry season, the clouds he hoped would hold more than promises of rain. "There's a new fire station," he told me in one of our phone conversations. He described its site in a former pasture now dotted with homes. It was about a mile or two from his house and an advantage given the proximity of wildfire. Clearing brush was another preventative option for residents, along with careful controlled burns. A National Fire Plan study found landowners on forested acreage more likely to take an active role in fire management, their stakes in the outcome high. Living in the Southwest also taught John and me about fire danger, the risks within our own backyard.

We reached the summit marked by the microwave tower. With our view of the city dimmed from low-lying clouds, the sky stayed opaque as the future. Ken and I started our way back down the road and into the trees. Deeper on the trail, mature cedar stretched to the sky with younger alder lining the road, an array of trees in this maturing forest. I touched dry moss along the way, smelled the sometimes-murky air, the area prone to wildfire as anyplace else in the American West. In a few years, the Carlton Complex of Central Washington, a wildfire of 250,000 acres, would become the largest wildfire in state history, fire danger not relegated to a single season. John and I offered our own unknowns, among them where we'd head next, a balance of our vocations with the places we loved best.

At the switchback where I'd stopped for breath on the way up, clouds now hid Mount Rainer, though its outline stayed close. The smell of smoke disappeared, whether I'd grown used to it or the haze lessened, I couldn't be certain. The only sure thing was the mountain's quiet shifts through changeable weather or additions to protected lands, its journey toward old growth secure as ours for now.

Epilogue

On a path weaving between Douglas fir, John and I hiked Squak Mountain from an access point a few miles away from Dad's house. On New Year's Day, the parking lot at the state park entrance was close to full from other like-minded hikers deciding to start their year outdoors. Wintry sunshine lit up the soft dirt of the trail with switchbacks so gentle we barely noticed the climb. I brushed my hand over a clump of moss, separating its individual tendrils. A trio of hikers passed us on their way down, their puppy stopping to sniff our shoes. Another couple passing us on a narrow turn wished us a Happy New Year. I breathed in cedar and listened to a creek rumbling down a ravine on its way to the valley and Issaquah Creek. We stepped off the path on a steep turn flanked by a stand of alder to let a horse and rider pass by, the horse's warm scent lingering. In single file on the narrowing trail, John and I kept a steady pace. I wasn't sure how far we'd hike today, if the summit was within reach or if we'd find a new route on this first day of the year.

Wearing hiking shoes and thick socks, our footsteps thumped across wooden bridges constructed for the park and turned silent again on a trail worn smooth from a mix of boots, sneakers, and hoof prints. Crumbling leaves from big leaf maple, fall remembrances from the year before, blended into the dirt and ferns on the sides of the path. On this last sunny day before rainy weather returned, the air felt sharp enough for the hat and gloves I wore, the hemlock trees along the trail wearing moss on their outstretched branches like long sleeves. In the middle of our second Midwest winter, this walk in thirty degree weather felt more temperate than it might have. Despite the chill of the last few days here, spring would return in a few months, and with it a move back to the Northwest.

The past decade, John and I had moved to places based on an American mix of jobs, family, and adventure, a journey taking us from Austin to West Texas for me and Minnesota for John, back to Austin, and then Wisconsin. Our next move followed John's new job and my heart, an opportunity to bring you home, John said. Starting in spring, John and I would pack our household, something we were good at by now, with John and the dog in a U-Haul and me in the car with our cat and good friend Hilary. Starting from the Midwest, we'd travel west through Minnesota, South Dakota, the corner of Wyoming, Montana, and Idaho until we reached eastern Washington. It would probably seem like any other road trip until the gradual climb up Snoqualmie Pass sank in, its steep drop on the other side pulling us back to trees outlined in moss and rain tapping the rooftops at night.

Partway up Squak, light angled through the tops of the trees. The mountain was deceptive that way, telling us *almost there* when we still had plenty of ground to cover. Familiar as the region was, we'd need to relearn certain parts of it, just as we'd bring our own perspectives from other places. The hometown I'd return to was no longer small, making Seattle seem even closer, its Space Needle view from the top of Squak Mountain coming into sharper relief. Thanks to protection of the mountain summit and surrounding lands, this particular park felt the same as it had years ago, the most visible differences well-kept trails skirting its sides and trees maturing toward old growth. New additions to public lands, such as King County's 2015 purchase of more than two hundred acres on Squak Mountain from a logging company, helped preserve habitat for the area's salmon and wildlife, along with offering recreational opportunities for the public. Despite the continuity of this and other landscapes, water quality, wildlife habitat, and wildfire management would require ongoing vigilance as the area grew, balancing living in a place with preserving its essential qualities one of the most important challenges of all.

We reached the mountain's midway point marked by a wooden sign and options. A path to the right led through the trees toward the gravel road twisting up the mountain; a path in the other direction crossed several more creeks and a ravine before ending up at Dad's. "We could walk right to his house from here," I said. John nodded, although both of us knew we wouldn't head to his house from the trail, not this particular walk. The gravel switchbacks up to the top would also wait for another time. For now, we turned around, retracing our steps toward the Trooper on the valley floor. With the air shadowed and growing cooler, we didn't pass as many people on the way down. Sunlight dusted the trail gold, and the turns came faster now. Heading home in a roundabout way made a good start to the year, a familiar place viewed in a different light.

Acknowledgments

Thanks to Andy Wilkinson for including this work in the Voice in the America West series and for his steadfast support. Thanks to Texas Tech University Press and to Joanna Conrad and Judith Keeling for giving this work a home. Thanks to Candice Adams Roma for her close read of the manuscript. Thanks to Dennis Covington, Jill Patterson, Toni Jensen, J. Marcus Weekley, and Mayanne Wright for their close reads and friendship. Thanks to the San Juan Workshops and Jill Patterson and the Conference on the Sowell Family Collection and Diane Warner for opportunities to share excerpts of this work. Thanks to the Artsmith Artist Residency. Thanks to Hilary Kaufmann, Johnnie Sielbeck, and Lori Steinhauer for their friendship and support. Thanks to Ken Folkins for countless hikes and to Delores Powers for her Northwest writing and memories. Thanks to William Folkins for his expertise in genealogy and family stories, his sharp remembrances, and for the many trips home. Thanks to John Koehler for sharing the journey.

"Blackberry Summers" appeared in *Caesura*; "Upstream" in Imagination and Place Press; "A Palouse Horse" in *Iron Horse Literary Review*; "Bigfoot in the Backyard" in *Fearsome Fascinations*; "Light in the Trees" in *Amoskeag: The Journal of Southern New Hampshire University*; "After the Volcano" in *R-KV-R-Y*.

Works Consulted and for Further Reading

Andrews, Ralph W. *This Was Logging*. Seattle, WA: Superior Publishing Co., 1954.

Appaloosa Museum and Heritage Center Foundation. "Appaloosa Museum." 2008. http://appaloosamuseum.org/.

Armstrong, Colleen Smith. "Search for 'Barefoot Burglar' Continues." *The Islands' Sounder*, March 3, 2010: 1.

"Ash eruption and fallout." *USGS*. June 1997. http://pubs.usgs.gov/gip/msh/ash.html.

Barber, Mike. "In Seconds, a Mountain and Many Lives Were Lost." *Seattle PI*, May 8, 2000.

Barfoot, Robyn. Personal Interview, Cougar Mountain Zoo. September 2009.

"Barton Springs Pool." Austin Parks and Recreation, *AustinTex.gov*, 2012. https://www.austintexas.gov/department/barton-springs-pool.

Beals, Harold O. and Terry C. Davis. "Figure in Wood." *Auburn University News and Publications*, January 1977.

Becker, Paula. "Pierce County—Thumbnail History." *History Link.org*, November 13, 2006. http://www.historylink.org/index.cfm?DisplayPage=output.cfm&file_id=8001.

Black, Anne E., Eva Strand, Penelope Morgan, J. Michael Scott, R. Gerald Wright, and Cortney Watson. "Biodiversity and Land-use History of the Palouse Bioregion: Pre-European to Present." *Land Use History of North America*. US Department of the Interior, December 2012. http://landcover.usgs.gov/luhna/chap10.php.

Bluemink, Elizabeth. "Federal agency calls for major work on trans-Alaska Pipeline." *Alaska Dispatch News*, February 11, 2011. http://www.adn.com/article/20110211/federal-agency-calls-major-work-trans-alaska-pipeline.

Brandstrom, Axel J. F. "Development of Industrial Forestry in the Pacific Northwest: The Colonel William B. Greeley Lectures in Industrial Forestry." University of Washington College of Forestry, Seattle, WA. Spring 1957: 16.

Broom, Jack. "Windstorm Prompts PSE Changes," December 14, 2007. http://www.seattletimes.com/seattle-news/windstorm-prompts-pse-changes/?syndication=rss.

"Connor Creek Erosion Control." Grays Harbor County Departments of Public Services, n.d. http://www.co.grays-harbor.wa.us/info/pub_svcs/Connor-Creek/index.html.

"Cougars (Mountain Lions)." *Living with Wildlife: Washington Department of Fish and Wildlife*, 2005. http://wdfw.wa.gov/living/cougars.html.

"Discovery Park's cougar is captured, released into wild." *Seattle Times*, September 8, 2009. http://www.seattletimes.com/seattle-news/discovery-parks-cougar-is-captured-released-into-wild/.

Dizon, Kirsten and May Bud. "Mount St. Helens from the Ashes." *Seattle PI*, May 2000.

"DNR Releases Taylor Bridge Fire Investigation." *Washington State Department of Natural Resources*, December 17, 2012. http://www.dnr.wa.gov/RecreationEducation/News/Pages/2012_12_17_taylor_nr.aspx.

Egan, Timothy. *The Good Rain: Across Time and Terrain in the Pacific Northwest*. New York: Vintage, 1991.

"Endangered Species Act Status of Puget Sound Killer Whales." *NOAA Fisheries: West Coast Region*, n.d. http://www.westcoast.fisheries.noaa.gov/protected_species/marine_mammals/killer_whale/esa_status.html.

Endejan, Kevin and Celeste Gracey. "From Fry to Figurehead." *Issaquah/Sammamish Reporter*, September 14, 2012.

"Fact Sheet On: The Chena Geothermal Power Plant." Chena Hot Springs Resort, n.d. http://gpw.alaskaenergy.govtools.us/documents/supportDocuments/Factsheets.pdf.

"Final Acquisition Set for Squak Mountain Forest, with King County—the Trust for Public Land Accord." *Natural Resources and Parks, King County*, March 31, 2014. http://www.kingcounty.gov/depts/dnrp/newsroom/newsreleases/2014/March/03-31-Squak-celebration.aspx.

"Flood Recovery Status One Year Later." *Mount Rainier National Park Fact Sheet*, November 2, 2007. http://www.nps.gov/mora/learn/news/upload/Flood%20Recovery%20Status%2011-2-07%20V1.pdf.

Folkins, William H. Personal Interview. 2008, 2012.

———. *Some Ancestors of Virginia M. Deisler*. Issaquah: Self-Published, n.d.

Gilman Town Hall Museum. "In this Valley: The Story of Our Town." Issaquah, Washington. Permanent Exhibit.

Gregory, James N. "Toward a History of Farm Workers in Washington State – Farm Workers in Washington State History Project." *Seattle Civil Rights and Labor History Project*, 2009. http://depts.washington.edu/civilr/farmwk_ch1.htm.

"Harriet Fish Named to 'Hall of Fame.'" *The Issaquah Press*, May 11, 1988: 3.

"History of the Issaquah Salmon Hatchery." *Friends of the Issaquah Salmon Hatchery*, 2014. http://www.issaquahfish.org/about-fish/history-of-the-issaquah-salmonhatchery/.

Holland, Mary Bailey Hall. "My Memories (1960)." In *Some Ancestors of Virginia M. Deisler*, edited by William H. Folkins. Issaquah: Self-Published, n.d.

Huggins, David R., and John P. Reganold. "No Till: the Quiet Revolution." *Scientific American*, July 2008: 70–78.

"I-90—Snoqualmie Pass East History." *Washington State Department of Transportation History*, 2015. http://www.wsdot.wa.gov/Projects/I90/SnoqualmiePassEast/History.htm.

Issaquah, Washington: Issaquah Historical Society. Chicago: Arcadia Publishing, 2002.

Kantor, Sylvia. "Moving Toward Sustainable Farming Practices." *Agriculture and Natural Resources Fact Sheet #533*. Cooperative Extension Washington State University King County. 1999.

Koehler, John. Personal Interview. 2012.

Koenninger, Tom, ed. *Mount St. Helens Holocaust: A Diary of Destruction*. Lubbock, TX: C. F. Boone Publishers Inc., 1980.

Lacitis, Eric, and Susan Gilmore. "December Wind Storm Now Dubbed the Hanukkah Eve Storm." *The Seattle Times*, March 2, 2007. http://www.seattletimes.com/seattle-news/december-wind-storm-now-dubbed-the-hanukkah-eve-storm/.

"Major in Organic Agriculture Systems." *Agricultural and Food Systems*. Washington State University, 2012. http://afs.wsu.edu/majors/organic-ag-systems/.

"Managing Wildfire Risk in Fire-Prone Landscapes: How Are Private Landowners Contributing?" *Science Findings* 154 (July 2013). http://www.fs.fed.us/pnw/sciencef/scifi154.pdf.

McDermott, Mark. "Phantom of the Woods, Phantom of the Psyche." *Pacific Magazine: The Seattle Times*, July 7, 1996: 10–14.

Michaud, Stephen G, and Hugh Aynesworth. *The Only Living Witness: The True Story of Serial Sex Killer Ted Bundy*. Irving, TX: Authorlink Press, 1999.

Moulton, Candy. *Chief Joseph: Guardian of the People*. New York: Tom Doherty Associates, 2005.

"Mount St. Helens—From the 1980 Eruption to 2000." *US Geological Survey—Reducing the Risk from Volcano Hazards Fact Sheet*. *USGS*. March 2000. http://pubs.usgs.gov/fs/2000/fs036-00/fs036-00.pdf.

Murphy, Michael. "Nez Perce Launch Horse Breeding Program." *Nez Perce Horse Registry*, November 1995. http://www.nezpercehorseregistry.com/11-95.html.

"National American Indian Heritage Month." Snoqualmie Falls, King County, Washington. *National Register of Historic Places*, November 2010. http://www.nps.gov/nr/feature/indian/2010/snoqualmie_falls.htm.

Nelson, Sharlene, and Ted Nelson. *Bull Whackers to Whistle Punks*. London: Franklin Watts, 1996.

Nerburn, Kent. *Chief Joseph and the Flight of the Nez Perce*. New York: HarperCollins, 2005.

"November 2006 Flood." Mount Rainier National Park. *National Park Service*,

April 2007. http://www.nps.gov/mora/learn/news/november-2006-flood-old-page.htm.

"Organic Dryland Farming: Eastern Washington and Northwestern Montana." *GoodFood World*, December 9, 2011. http://www.goodfoodworld.com/2011/12/organic-dryland-farming-eastern-washington-and-northwestern-montana/.

Ott, Jen. "Aberdeen—Thumbnail History." *History Link.org*, November 2, 2009. http://www.historylink.org/index.cfm?DisplayPage=output.cfm&file_id=7390.

Patent, Dorothy Hinshaw. *Appaloosa Horses*. New York: Holiday House, 1988.

Pittock, Barrie. "From Academic Science to Political Hot Potato: Climatic Change, Risk, and Policy Relevance." *Climatic Change*, May 20, 2010. http://link.springer.com/article/10.1007/s10584-010-9819-4.

Powers, Delores. Personal Interview. 2011, 2012.

Raftery, Isolde. "'Barefoot Bandit' Gets Prison for Stealing from Neighbors." *The New York Times*, December 17, 2011. http://www.nytimes.com/2011/12/17/us/colton-harris-moore-the-barefoot-bandit-is-sentenced-for-stealing-from-neighbors.html?_r=0.

"Review of 2012: Climatic Averages and the Top 7 Weather Events." *Office of the Washington State Climatologist Newsletter* vol 7 issue 2, February 4, 2013: 5. http://www.climate.washington.edu/newsletter/2013Feb.pdf.

Rule, Ann. *The Stranger Beside Me*. New York: W. W. Norton, 2000.

"Ryderwood, Washington." *Firewise*, 2014. http://firewise.org/wildfire-preparedness/be-firewise/success-stories/washington/ryderwood-washington.aspx?sso=0.

Serling, Robert J. *Legend and Legacy: The Story of Boeing and its People*. New York: St. Martin's Press, 1992.

"Southern Resident Killer Whales: 10 Years of Research and Conservation." NOAA Fisheries, June 2014. http://www.nwfsc.noaa.gov/news/features/killer_whale_report/pdfs/bigreport62514.pdf.

Southwest Washington Coastal Erosion Study. US Geological Survey Coastal and Marine Geology Program, n.d. http://www.ecy.wa.gov/programs/sea/swces/.

Squak Mountain State Park. *Washington State Parks*, n.d. http://www.parks.wa.gov/588/Squak-Mountain.

"*S.S. Catala* Shipwreck Oil Removal Project Final Update, September 2007." *Department of Ecology State of Washington*, September 2007. http://www.ecy.wa.gov/programs/spills/incidents/catala/factsheet_092007.pdf.

Stokes, Robert. "Salmon Are Not Created Equal." *Inlander*, November 21, 2001. http://www.inlander.com/spokane/salmon-are-not-created-equal/Content?oid=2126419.

Sullivan, Jennifer. "Teen Criminal Suspected of Striking Again on Orcas Island."

Seattle Times, February 28, 2010. http://www.seattletimes.com/seattle-news/teen-criminal-suspected-of-striking-again-on-orcas-island/.

Sykes, Karen. "Time to take a closer look at nearby Squak Mountain." *Seattle Post Intelligencer*, March 28, 2001. http://www.seattlepi.com/news/article/Time-to-take-a-closer-look-at-nearby-Squak-1050944.php.

32-Horse Drawn Rumley Combine, 1938. Whitman County Heritage. Washington State Library, November 19, 2010. http://content.statelib.wa.gov/cdm/printview/collection/whitman/id/2690/type/singleitem.

Thorsen, Kim. "Public Safety, Resource Protection, and Emergency Services Department of the Interior Before Senate Committee on Energy and Natural Resources Concerning Preparedness for the 2013 Fire Season," June 4, 2013. http://www.energy.senate.gov/public/index.cfm/files/serve?File_id=803a6eff-2ba6-477f-ba0e-68d163592e9c.

Tweed, Katherine. "World's Highest Wind Turbine Will Hover Above Alaska." *IEEE Spectrum*, March 25, 2012. http://spectrum.ieee.org/energywise/energy/renewables/first-commercial-floating-wind-turbine-hovers-above-alaska.

"2008 United States National Seismic Hazard Map." *USGS*, April 2008. http://pubs.usgs.gov/fs/2008/3018/pdf/FS08-3018_508.pdf.

"Vineyards." *Salmon Safe*, 2012. http://www.salmonsafe.org/getcertified/vineyards.

"Volcanic Landslides at Mount Rainier Volcano, Washington." *Volcano Hazards Program USGS*, December 29, 2009. http://volcanoes.usgs.gov/hazards/landslide/rainier.php.

"Washaway Beach." *Washington's Coast*. Washington State Department of Ecology, n.d. http://www.ecy.wa.gov/programs/sea/coast/erosion/washaway.html.

"WDFW officers tracking cougar that reportedly attacked child in Stevens County." Washington Department of Fish and Wildlife, September 3, 2009. http://wdfw.wa.gov/news/sep0309b/.